Magic & Miracles & Goodness

No Tree! No Toys! No Toot Toot!

A Heartwarming story of a nineteen-month-old Christmas disappeared while he was napping

---

This is a true story about a nineteen-month-old, who saw it all disappear after a several hour afternoon nap. Everything was gone. The tree, the train, all the toys and even the platform where everything was displayed.

Christmas was the way it was every year, but this was only little Brian's second Christmas. He loved every part of the holidays. Every day from the day mom and dad put it all up, he would run the train for hours with his daddy. After Christmas he enjoyed the tree and the beautiful platform and a ton of toys from Santa. He felt like it was magical. He did not remember much about his first Christmas when he was seven months old. But nothing that first year ever gave him a feeling like he got on this particular day. It was all gone.

What now? Now that everything was gone? In this book you will learn the preliminaries that happened before Christmas 1981 and you will learn how the young boy in the story survived to enjoy many future Christmases. This is a true story and poetic license was just a small part of telling the whole true story

Even if you do not believe in Santa, who deep down we all know exists and lives in the North Pole, you will love this story. It's like as if Santa is working even when it is not Christmas Eve to help every child be a better child and to be able to smile whenever possible.

This is great family reading. A real family is highlighted in this fine uplifting story. Thank you for reading it. You can read this book to all your children and their friends and they will love it. Enjoy! Have a great and magical day. I have a feeling that the tree, the toys, and the toot-toot will all be back next year if not sooner.

BRIAN W. KELLY

Copyright © Nov. 2018, Brian W. Kelly   Publisher: Brian P. Kelly
Title: No Tree; No Toys; No Toot Toot.   Author: Brian W. Kelly
Subtitle: A heartwarming story of a nineteen month-old. Christmas disappeared while he was napping.

All rights reserved: No part of this book may be reproduced or transmitted in any form, or by any means, electronic or mechanical, including photocopying, recording, scanning, faxing, or by any information storage and retrieval system, without permission from the publisher, LETS GO PUBLISH, in writing.

Disclaimer: Though judicious care was taken throughout the writing and the publication of this work, that the information contained herein is accurate, there is no expressed or implied warranty that all information in this book is 100% correct. Therefore, neither LETS GO PUBLISH nor the author accepts liability for any use of this work.

Trademarks: A number of products and names referenced in this book are trade names and trademarks of their respective companies.

Referenced Material: *Standard Disclaimer:* *The information in this book has been obtained through personal and third party observations, interviews, and copious research. Where unique information has been provided or extracted from other sources, those sources are acknowledged within the text of the book itself or at the end of the chapter in the Sources Section. Thus, there are no formal footnotes nor is there a bibliography section. Any picture that does not have a source was taken from various sites on the Internet with no credit attached. If resource owners would like credit in the next printing, please email publisher.*

Published by: LETS GO PUBLISH!
Publisher   Brian P. Kelly
Email: info@letsgopublish.com
Web site   www.letsgopublish.com

Library of Congress Copyright Information Pending
Book Cover Design by Brian W. Kelly
Editor— Brian P. Kelly

ISBN Information: The International Standard Book Number (ISBN) is a unique machine-readable identification number, which marks any book unmistakably. The ISBN is the clear standard in the book industry. 159 countries and territories are officially ISBN members. The Official ISBN For this book is on the outside cover: **ISBN 9781947402669**

The price for this work is:								$9.95 USD	
10	9	8	7	6	5	4	3	2	1
Release Date:								November 2016	

Publisher's Note: *Please check out www.letsgopublish.com to read the latest version of our heartfelt acknowledgments updated for this book. On the site, please click the bottom item of the Main menu!*

Dedication

Special Thanks Are Extended:

To the little Chile Beans in this story, Brian Kelly, Mike Kelly, Katie Kelly, and Dawn Boyle.

You all have been bugging me for years to write a book such as this.

I hope you like it!

Thank you all for being so kind!

Other books are available at amazon.com/author/brianwkelly

My name is:

_____
Write your name here:

Table of Contents

Chapter 1 The People in this Christmas Story 1

Chapter 2 Mom and Dad's Honeymoon! 13

Chapter 3 Breezie, Our First Doggie! 21

Chapter 4 Life on 47 Perfect Street 41

Chapter 5 The Stork Brings Me to Perfect Street 51

Chapter 6 Baby Brian's First Christmas--1980 73

Chapter 7 St. Patrick's Day and Easter 1981 83

Chapter 8 The Summer of 1981 89

Chapter 9 The Fall of 1981 99

Chapter 10 Baby Brian's Second Christmas 105

Chapter 11 After Christmas 1981—A New Brother! 119

Chapter 12 Life Goes On! 127

Other Books by Brian W. Kelly: (amazon.com, and Kindle) 137

Chapter 1 The People in this Christmas Story

The picture above shows where our family lived—47 Perfect Street. Forty-Nine was the left half of the white double block and Forty-Seven (our home) was on the right. In this picture, the house was dressed for Halloween. Below is an ad for a Theatre in our hometown.

The English Tudor home on the right side is where the Bee family and Dawn Pavlov lived. Dawn and I are the same age and she was my best friend on Perfect Street.

The Bees had moved in right next door on the left side of the Tudor at 45 Perfect St. and the Pavlovs lived at 43 Perfect Street.

These two homes were at the top of the hill on Perfect Street. If we went left or right from these homes, the hills were steep. As kids, our big wheels came in very handy. It was a long haul back up the hills, after the great ride down, however, Now as I think back, it was dangerous—but nobody ever got hurt.

I'm not only the person telling everybody who reads this the big story about Brian P. Kells. I am your narrator, Brian Patrick Kells II and I am happy to meet you all. I am also the major character in this story. I am a lot older now than when this story happened on Perfect Street in our hometown at the time of Wilkes-Barre PA.

I have the distinct pleasure of telling this phenomenally incredible story about me, my brother Mikey and my sister Katie and a bunch of other wonderful people. I already have two pages finished.

The facts in this story come mostly from me but Mikey and Katie also provided a lot of insights about what was going on at our Perfect Street residence.

Some other facts and stories recalled come from my mom—Patricia Trosk Kells, my dad—Brian W. Kells, Sr. and my grandparents: Pop— "Smokey" Trosk; Nana—Arlene "Skippo" Trosk; Pop—Edward J. Kells; and Nana—Irene "Grandma Biddie" Kells.

Most of this story is true though I do add a few extra facts of my own as I am the main character in the story. But, first of course, I had to be born. Others in the story are uncle Joseph Kells and aunt Diane Kells; Uncle Bill Danells and aunt Mary Danells. Of course there is also my dad's big brother, uncle Ed "Eudart" Kells, and his big sister, aunt Nancy Flanders .

I can't wait to tell you this story.

In case you miss it, which I don't think you will— the Kells and the Trosks were big Christmas people. We still are.

By the way, that big white house on the first page was really, really big. It was a double block with eight rooms on each side. The left side had two four-room apartments and the right side was an eight-room half-double.

Before I was born, my mom and dad lived on the left side of the house on the second floor in a four-room apartment. It had a kitchen, a living room and two bedrooms. Mom and dad slept in one bedroom and they used the other bedroom as a dining-room.

Grandpop Edward J Kells, also known as Pop Kells, lived down the street at 18 Perfect Street. When dad and mom bought the big house on Perfect Street in 1975, it cost them $21,000 but it needed a lot of work as Pop Kells, who did most of the work, often said. All that work was done well before I was born,

Pop Kells promised my dad, his son, Brian W. Kells, that he would do whatever was needed to fix up the house on the inside. There were some holes in the walls and ceilings plus the whole place—all eight rooms (four downstairs and four upstairs plus one bath) needed to be repainted.

Pop Kells decided that as soon a mom and dad came back from their honeymoon, he would get started on the job. So, while they were gone, he went to Main Hardware and got all of the supplies that he would need.

I, Brian P. Kells II am the first-born child of Brian Sr. and Patricia Kells. I made my first appearance on May 28, 1980. I'll tell you all about that after a few more chapters.

For now, let me say that on the day I was born, it was a very nice day in our hometown in Pennsylvania. The summer was about to come, and it was a hot one.

My mom and dad had a pool and they needed it with me continually squawking in the shade of the back porch on Perfect street.

About nineteen months later on December 30, 1981, right after Christmas and before New Years Eve, my brother Mikey was born. The neighbors called us Irish twins. Cold as it might have been, it was a warm day for dad and mom --and their nineteen month-old-son —me.

My sister Kate waited longer to be born but I am glad she finally appeared almost three years later on November 12, 1984. She was a beauty as I recall and my mom and dad were thrilled to have a baby girl.

Let me show you a picture of the three Kells kids some time around 1987. The picture was taken at Pop Kells house at 18 Perfect Street.

From left to right, Me—Brian, Dad, Mikey, Mom, & Katie

My dad, Brian Sr. still is a jokester. He chortled about having Irish twins right after Mikey was born. He said that if the Kells had the good fortune to have triplets, he would have named the third baby Jesus—pronounced Hey Zeus and might have named the other two, Joseph and Mary.

But, Kate came when both Mikey and I were buzzing around the house and both of us could make it up and down the steps.

For the record, mom did not find Dad's jokes amusing at all. Our family was always very religious and my dad loved the idea of Jesus, Mary & Joseph being born in his family.

However, mom had a tough time thinking about real triplets. I guess Mikey and I were a lot of work, but we always knew we were well loved.

Life was especially good for our family. Dad had a great job with IBM and mom was a teacher by trade when Mikey and I came so quickly after no children for five years. Mom sacrificed to stay home and help me grow up. Mom and dad decided that mom would stay at home to make sure all us kids grew up right.

As I said, Grandpop and Grandma Kells lived right down the street. Additionally, when the Bees moved in next door in the Tudor house on the right, they became best friends with our family. Dawn and I were the same age.

Mom and Dad originally planned to stay on Perfect Street for a few years and then move to a single home. But there were too many good reasons to stay a lot longer. The family lived there thirteen years. I lived there eight years.

Mom and dad had bought the Perfect St. home in 1975 right before they got married. Rather than pay rent, Pop Kells fixed up the two-four-room units on the left side of the block. It was a nice place.

Pop also fixed up the big eight room half-double and life was very good for all of us. Mom and dad rented-out both apartments when they moved to the half-double

All of the members of the family were healthy as were the Bees next door. That's all that really mattered to the Kells.

When I was born and Mikey and Katie, we had a big enough house to have our own bedrooms. But, Mikey and I shared a room with bunkbeds because Dad needed to have an office.

Dad said that for years while they were waiting for the stork after they moved to the half-double side, they picked the front bedroom. Right after the move, they bought a queen-sized bed. They moved their bed from the apartment into the middle bedroom which eventually became Katie's bed.

Moving to the back of the house, the next bedroom (Katie's) was unused. Dad first took the bedroom at the top of the steps. It had a diagonal door entrance right at the top of the front steps. It was perfect for his office. It was a nice sized bedroom.

The next bedroom was down the hall next to the bathroom. It was the fourth bedroom right after a set of back steps. Yes, there were two sets of steps to get up and down the first and second floors.

When we, the three kids were all born, Katie got the second bedroom and Pop Kells painted it white with one pink wall. They put in a matching pink carpet also.

The back bedroom was the guest room before Mikey and Katie came along. I first slept in the crib in what became Katie's room. When Mikey came, they moved all of dad's office stuff into the back bedroom and Mikey and I got to share his former office.

Mom and dad bought a couple dressers and a bunk bed. I got the top bunk and Mikey got the bottom. It was great.

Here is what the downstairs looked like.

When mom and dad got back from their honeymoon and dad was finally OK, he went back to work at IBM and mom went back to work at the Bureau for the Visually Handicapped.

Pop Kells religiously came to the house every morning and worked 'til about 2:00 pm before he left for home down at 18 Perfect Street. He really did a lot of work.

Four rooms upstairs and four rooms downstairs to paint. He patched the holes in the plaster and painted and painted and painted. Dad learned how to do wall-papering and he papered all but the ceiling in the kitchen. Pop Kells patched the ceilings and painted them white. He also patched the walls so dad could wallpaper them.

The wallpaper dad used in the kitchen was very patriotic--red white and blue with sayings from the American Revolution. I remember it was very upbeat. Pop also painted the background for the kitchen stove black as well as the stovepipes. He made it real nice.

He also used a special black material to bring back the color from the Wilkes-Barre coal stove we had in the kitchen. Here is a cut out picture of the back door to show how dad painted the new duct work black to match the black kitchen stove that was off to the right.

Take a look on the next page and you will see one of the only other pictures of the kitchen I could find that has that special wall-paper. That's me in 1982 with my three-month-old brother Mikey.

Mom worked hard in the kitchen lining the cupboards with special sticky paper after Pop had painted the outside and the inside of the cupboards. She made it real nice as I recall.

To go with the patriotic theme, Pop painted the kitchen door and the cellar door and an antique red color that matched the wallpaper.

Everybody loved the look of the kitchen.

Coming in the front door, Dad wallpapered the entire left side of the house. With the open staircase the wall went all the way up to the second-floor ceiling.

Dad papered the other side of the hallway upstairs also from the front bedroom to the bathroom in the rear. He also papered one wall in what became my room and it was beautiful.

The last wall that he papered was downstairs in the dining room. It was tropical flowery and matched the green rug that mom bought for that room.

The third room by the kitchen from where you would walk in from the front door was not wall-papered but Pop Kells did panel the far wall. He painted the three walls gold. Mom put a gold la-z-boy chair in there that matched perfectly

Pop patched and painted all of the walls that were not painted a nice shade of white. He painted one wall in Katie's room pink and it matched the rug that we got for that room.

Eventually pop was done and mom and dad moved in about four years before I was born. It took Pop Kells about five months to finish all the work. Meanwhile, mom and dad lived in the second-floor apartment on the left side of the big white house on Perfect Street.

Perfect Street was a great place to live. Let me go back in time now to the period in which Mom and Dad had just gotten married after buying the big house on Perfect Street. It is a great story about how life together began for mom and dad. It is the unique story of their honeymoon. Only Hollywood in the days of John Wayne movies could top this story. I hope you like it.

Chapter 2 Mom and Dad's Honeymoon!

I heard this story a thousand times and I like hearing it every time. Mom and Dad came back from the honeymoon at Mount Airy Lodge early because dad got hurt doing the organized athletics at the resort. Below is a nice picture of the resort.

Dad told me that on the second day, Monday, they played tennis, then they played softball, and then in the afternoon, they went for a long horseback ride with a group. There is a picture at the resort that Mom showed me with dad's head bent over like his chin was in his chest. He said he could not move his head or neck. He looked like he was in pain because he was.

Dad said he was not sure what was wrong but expected to feel better soon. There was a picture taken when Dad and Mom were getting ready to go in for their evening meal. You could see dad's head tilted downwards. I could not find that picture for this story.

When mom and dad got to the table after the athletic day, they were with the same group of friends from the night before. Mom told them that dad was a little sore and Dad did his best to show no pain. He said the red wine at dinner really helped him.

The dinner was delicious, both mom and Dad agreed. They had steak and scallops and a great chocolate cake with thick icing for dessert. After dinner, they had a few cocktails with their new friends and then everybody decided to cash it in for the night.

Dad was getting a bit stiffer and the pain was increasing as he walked the lengthy halls back to the room. The bed was comfortable, but Dad's neck was really hurting.

At Midnight, the pain got so bad the hotel security, Mount Airy Lodge, at mom's request called an ambulance and they took Dad to the Monroe County General Hospital Emergency room. That's the part of the story where everybody normally has a big laugh.

The hospital took X-rays and saw that nothing was broken. They told dad in a few days the inflammation would die down and he would feel much better.

Dad set his watch for 48 hours. He counted the hours. Dad and mom went back to the hotel and Dad finally got to sleep. They gave Dad some strong pills, but he says even today that the pills did nothing that first night.

As we discussed, mom and dad met some nice people the first day and when they went to dinner the second day after dad hurt himself, as noted above, they sat with the same people. The hotel had made table assignments and every day. They were the same.

When Dad hurt himself on Monday, after he went to dinner, and the hospital, he could no longer get out of bed. That was it for dad for meeting people for dinner. Dad said he was in pain all week long even after the 48 hours and it hurt just to move.

I remember hearing dad tell the story lots of times but when mom told it, it took a lot longer and she made it seem funny. Whenever they got to the part where on their honeymoon, dad was not allowed to move from Tuesday through Thursday **on his honeymoon,** the people listening always enjoyed that no matter who told the story—they always had one heck of a belly laugh.

Even Uncle Joe and Uncle Ed who heard the account a number of times over the years, could not hold in their laughter. Dad always seemed to know the big laugh was coming at the same spot in the story, so he got used to it and it did not seem to bother him so much.

Mom says that it really did bother him a lot, but he would sound like a wuss if he complained. She loved making the story go longer to get dad's goat.

Dad said she made things up over the years. I am not sure who I believe. I did not think the story was really funny. Over the years, the story became easier for dad to tell but mom would always cut him off to make sure every detail was covered.

Dad said mom was very nice while he lay incapacitated in their huge King-Size bed at Mount Airy Resort in the Poconos. She said the bed had a big mirror on the ceiling and this bugged dad as he got to see how much in pain he actually was.

Dad said there were three bright spots for him every day. Breakfast, Lunch, and Dinner. Then he would say "That's It! That's all there was—even the TV stations were lousy."

If he thought mom would go for it, dad told me he might have asked for a late-night snack, but he knew he was a burden. Having mom with him for meals was punishment enough for her as dad would say. Honeymoons were meant to be fun for both parties.

Mom was glad that she had met other couples and after Tuesday's lunch, she stayed with them at their invitation for their recreation events. They also saved a spot for her at all their meals.

They were all very nice and took mom wherever they were going, and she appreciated it. There was a lot to do but her partner, my dad, was down so she could not play in everything.

It did give her some of what she was missing from Dad being hurt and all. Because mom had begun to make do and if the truth be known, was actually beginning to have some fun, dad's meals got delivered later and later.

Mom enjoyed eating with the group of new friends. Dad said he did not mind but then again, he talked about it a lot like as if Mom was enjoying herself while he was not having any fun at all. He could not have been having fun.

Getting through Tuesday seemed like an eternity. Dad said he expected to feel better by the end of the day or perhaps the next, but he did not feel better.

Mom was not there for him to even complain to. He said often when recounting the Honeymoon, that even the TV shows were lousy and the pain made it hard to sleep. So, overall, it was pretty boring and miserable for Dad.

Wondering when dad would be OK had to make it very unpleasant for Mom too so neither of them were having a picnic. By the end of Tuesday dad felt worse. When Mom came with dinner at about 8:00PM it was cold but that was OK for dad.

He was glad mom was enjoying herself, really, and he felt he would be joining her soon. It did not happen.

The friends were going to a concert at the resort so mom went with them that night and again dad watched prime time TV. He hoped he would fall asleep and wake up better but there was little relief even the next day. Each day was the same.

On Friday when dad got up, he realized that on the coming Sunday they would be checking out and he was hoping Mom might agree to depart from the honeymoon early as he was still bedridden. He hoped to watch the weekend football games on his own TV at home.

Heading home

Dad could not drive because he could not keep his head upright for any length of time. He said it was like having an anvil for a head.

Dad's Volkswagen Bus was a stick shift and mom had never driven it. She called Uncle Joe who kindly agreed to come up to the Poconos by early afternoon on Friday to pick the two honeymooners up from their week of "fun."

It was about an hour ride from home. The shock absorbers on the "bus" were not so great nor was the condition of the roads and so dad felt every bump on the way home.

Dad knew that's how it would be, and he was not looking forward to the ride home. When Uncle Joe got there, Mom and the security team were able to get dad into the Volkswagen bus and they helped him lie down on the floor with a big pillow. Mom drove uncle Joe's car home and followed the "bus." It took about an hour, they said.

There were no cell phones back then so there was no talking between mom and uncle Joe on the way home. Before mom had called Joe that morning, she called Joshy Bohunk, a good friend. Mom and dad had just closed the mortgage on the house and nobody had lived in the home even one night before the honeymoon. There were no beds anyway.

While on the honeymoon, the bed arrived thankfully, and Pop Kells let the delivery people in to the apartment on the second floor on the left side of the building. When she called him, Mom asked Joshy Bohunk if he would assemble the bed and put the springs and mattress on it as dad could not lift anything.

Somehow dad says when he got into the house and up the stairs, the bed was all set up and somebody (*God love them*—dad's words) had put a sheet etc. on the new bed so all dad had to do was climb in.

He said he was a lot better--about 75% OK when he got into the bed. On that day, he does not remember much after that.

He fell asleep. He was home. He was a little better the next day and after about three more days, dad said he was functional with just a couple twinges of pain every now and then. He got some stronger medicine from Doctor Decker when he got home.

Uncle Franny Kurilla, his great friend had already carried the new refrigerator up the steps to the apartment. When Joshy Bohumk and uncle Joe got dad up the steps, they filled the refrigerator up with beer.

Mom and dad had not even gotten their first food order. Dad said that the beer plus a few nips of VO made everything else better until he was all better. The weekend football games made time go much faster.

On Monday, one week after hurting himself, Dad finally was able to move around. He went to the grocery store and bought a few things and for my mom and dad, their life together was about to begin.

Though the people at Mount Airy were nice and they did give a partial refund, mom and dad never ever got that honeymoon in the Poconos that they had planned for so long.

Maybe it is on their bucket list!

Chapter 3 Breezie, Our First Doggie!

Hello Doggy

My Aunt, Mary Danyells, had two beautiful dogs. One was named Burf, and the other was named Muggles. My dad called Muggles ***Bagel Wagel***. Both of the dogs were female.

Burf was the only puppy in a litter from Mrs. Beasely, my Aunt Nancy's dog. The other partner in all of these dog entanglements that produced offspring was a guy the family respectfully called "visitor."

Burf found her own visitor and she had a litter of beautiful puppies. When just two puppies were left, Aunt Mary, who knew my dad wanted a dog for their new family, brought two little five-week old rascals over to the second-floor apartment on Perfect Street.

Dad says he still remembers it like it was yesterday. He and mom were in the kitchen. The two puppies were sleepy tired but when my mom, Pat came into the room, dad said the little fur-balls came to life.

Mary set both puppies down on the kitchen floor and immediately the one who would be our puppy went to mom's feet and he laid down right on top of them and he just stayed there.

Dad was hoping mom would say that we could keep him. Mom was so taken back by the loving little guy she said yes even before she picked him up.

The other guy was cute too, but mom's heart was taken. Aunt Mary asked Aunt Nancy about the other puppy and she took him and called him Toby.

Mom decided to call our puppy Breezie. He had a name even before he lived with us. Mary said he needed another week or two more with Burf before she could bring him to the house for good. Dad was very excited.

The day came. The little guy was not trained so there were a lot of calls to go on the paper and there was a lot of poop in the upstairs apartment for the first few months of the little guy's life.

Mom and dad could not sleep with the little guy yelping at night so at some point they would take him over to the other side. Pop was working on that side every day so he was the first to greet Breezie every day about 7:00 AM.

Mom and dad were able to sleep, and pop made sure the little guy ate in the morning. Mom and dad went to work and when they came home the doggie joined them upstairs.

There were a lot of wet floors and stinky material on the floors during this training period. It seemed to last forever but mom and dad were in their twenties and were able to handle it well.

Big fear: Is Breezie going to die?

One morning when Pop Kells came to work on the house, Breezie was listless and all sweaty looking. Something was wrong. Pop got mom somehow and then she got dad.

Dad looked up veterinarians in the phone book and he found Dr. Colladay in Mountaintop, about ten miles away. He ran a Pet hospital. Mom made the call.

Dad checked out where Pop was working and found a can of turpentine with the paint brushes softening in it. The dog's breath and the smell of his facial fur gave it away. He had clearly drunk turpentine, which is a poison.

The doctor told mom to bring the dog right up. Before he left both mom and dad smelled more turpentine on the sticky fur by Breezie's mouth. He had definitely drunk turpentine. Would he live? There was a lot left in the can with the paint brushes so that part was good.

Dad and mom took him right up to the hospital and met with Dr. Colladay. The doctor knew the antidote and he did whatever else was in the book for turpentine poisoning.

By this time, it was getting dark and the doctor said he would keep him overnight and see if he could flush out the poison.

My mom and dad went home but before so, they were instructed to call back in the morning to see if Breezie made it through the night. Mom and dad said there was not much sleeping. And there was a lot of praying. He was just a puppy

Pop Kells, when informed, had to be convinced that it was not his fault. Pop had come to love the little guy like we all did. I did not know it then but Breezie would become my dog.

He made it. Mom made the call in the AM and Dr. Colladay said he was OK and he would be OK but the doctor asked if my parents would leave Breezie at the hospital for the rest of the day.

Dad and mom picked him up that early evening and his tail was wagging. Breezie had made it. Whew!

Life is good. That night he slept in the 2nd floor apartment and the next day his excretory markings were clearly visible. All systems were working.

One night in the hospital was not enough to train this little puppy to GO outside.

The Spider Plant and the Wall Incident

Dad tells the next best puppy story. After a few more months it was getting closer to Christmas. Mom and dad loved Christmas. I get it from them. I love Christmas.

Dad was working a little late in the IBM office in Scranton and he called mom at home to make sure everything was OK. It was not OK.

Mom was crying profusely, and she could hardly speak. She said "the dog ate my spider plant and then he pooped on the floor and he wiped his butt on the wall." She was very upset.

She added that Breezie then kicked up all the dirt onto the floor from the spider plant container. She then said for dad to get home as soon as possible. She said she did not want the dog anymore. The Dog had to go or mom said she would be going soon.

Dad was not sure what to do.

Though he had a lot more work to do, Dad chose not to spend any more time at IBM that night. He came right home. However, he did stop at Raves, a great garden store on his way home. IBM in Scranton was about 25 miles away from home.

Raves was a full-service gardening center with very nice plants. Dad bought a beautiful Spider Plant for mom—even better than the one that was formerly in a big pot full of dirt on the living room floor.

Mom was thrilled to get the new spider plant and she had already cleaned up the rug from the dog diggings. She was almost OK by the time dad got home.

However, she could not stand the fact that after the puppy had made such a monstrous poop, Breezie topped it off by wiping his butt on the wall right behind the new couch. Mom could hardly get the words out when dad came home.

It was all cleaned up but mom left the brown stain on the wall, so Dad could see it. Mom hoped that Dad too would get upset with the "bad" doggie and dad would agree the dog had to go.

Sure enough, as dad was forced to examine the wall, there were poop skid-marks right behind the new couch exactly where mom had said. Dad thought that no dog would ever do that on purpose.

Dad looked closer, expecting to generate some olfactory senses. The nose was not picking up anything. What else could be brown and not look like dirt?

Soon, dad found papers that said Krackel and Mr. Goodbar and Dark Chocolate on them, and he figured out the big mystery.

Breezie had dug up the spider plant for sure. His digging sprayed fresh dirt all over the white rug. He weighed so little the dirt was not mushed in. Mom used the broom and the sweeper and got it all up.

The mystery dad discovered was that the dog was attracted to the Hershey Miniature dish from the coffee table and he ripped a bunch of them open and devoured them.

Thankfully Breezie did not eat enough to make him sick. As you know, Dogs, should not eat chocolate. Mom and dad were lucky the doggie did not have another turpentine reaction.

In large enough amounts, chocolate and cocoa products can kill your dog. The toxic component of chocolate is theobromine.

Humans easily metabolize theobromine, but dogs process it much more slowly, allowing it to build up to toxic levels in their system. I am so glad Breezie made it twice.

With her new Spider Plant and with the mess cleaned up already, mom was a different person and not upset like she was on the phone. She loved the new plant and loved the dog again.

Dad showed her the candy paper trail and together, they concluded that the skid marks were chocolate drippings from the puppy's mouth and not poop. Breezie was eating the treats on top of the couch by the white wall with melted chocolate drooling from his mouth.

Mom and dad had a wonderful laugh and went to bed knowing the dog had a treat and mom had a great new plant.

Breezie: the Construction Worker

By Christmas Eve, Breezie was doing much better on the squeaking (very noisy) and his droppings were not as regular an occurrence. Mom had decorated the apartment for Christmas and dad said it was beautiful.

The pictures prove it. It was beautiful for sure. Pop was making great progress in remodeling the eight rooms next door and he had learned to push the dog droppings into a pile for dad to pick up each night. r

After resigning themselves to having two great Christmas turkey dinners, one at the Kells (mom and dad with Biddie and Pop Kells) and the other at the Trosks (mom and dad with Skippo and Pop Trosk), - my mom and dad went to bed in their queen-sized bed to get a good night sleep.

In the middle of the night, they were both awakened by the sound of construction. Hard as it is to believe, it was in the middle of the night.

What could it be?

There was pounding and there was also a gnawing sound. When mom and dad's bed was assembled by Joshy Bohunk, because the house was old, Joshy told mom and dad that he had to find some blocks of wood to even out the four posts of the bed so the bed by itself did not sway back and forth.

By this time late on Christmas Eve, mom and dad were awake. They realized that the construction sound was coming from under the bed. Surly the construction worker had to be wearing a hard hat. It was definitely not Santa.

But, who could it be as nobody but mom and dad and Breezie lived in the house along with a few small mice. Though prevalent in the Perfect Street neighborhood, the mice were never known to make such a racket.

Mom and dad looked at each other and they smiled. They realized it was the puppy teething. He was gnawing on the blocks of wood as puppies do but he was not squeaking as he was months earlier. The puppy was happy. They were gnaws of happiness.

FYI, a puppy's baby teeth start coming in between 3 to 5 weeks of age, and all their baby teeth are full grown by the time they're 8 weeks old. Breezie had all his baby teeth when he was under the bed.

At about ages 4 to 6 months, the process starts all over again, with a dog's adult teeth coming in. A puppy grows a total of 28 baby teeth—12 incisors, 4 canines and 12 premolars. In comparison to us humans, a puppy doesn't have his baby teeth for very long.

In just a month after he finishes growing them, a puppy starts losing his baby teeth. Eventually a dog has 42 teeth so the little furballs are growing teeth from about 3 weeks to about 26 weeks. That means that Breezie was working on his teeth under our bed on Christmas Eve. See the picture below of Breezie when he as five years old. Dad was holding him in this picture.

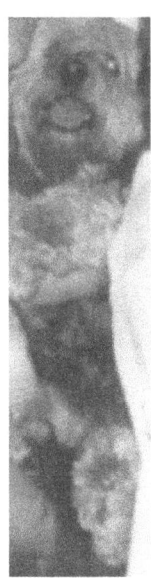

Eventually mom and dad caught on to the rhythm and woke up on Christmas morning with their new little man, Breezie, sound asleep under the bed. Mom and dad envisioned the little guy under the bed with a little hard hat on to make sure he got all his work done. They could not help laughing.

Breezie was as cute a dog as anybody could have ever met in life. The next morning my parents spotted some obvious bite marks in the blocks of wood.

Close by was a little wet spot and a few small logs so mom and dad had more proof that the little man's internal system was functioning well. The Kells had survived the construction activity

Chapter 4 The Puppy's Christmas & the March 1980 Move

Our two turkey dinners at Pop Kells and Pop Trosks on Christmas day were as picturesque as the picture above.

Pop Kells told mom and dad on Christmas day that he was doing so well on the construction work that he believed that by the end of January, he would be done, and they could make their move to the half-double.

Christmas dinner was great at Pop Kells at noon and it was great at Pop Trosks at 6:00 PM. Both the Trosks and the Kells loved Breezie. And, he was there at both stops that day to enjoy some turkey.

The night before Christmas—about 5:00 PM after mass on Christmas Eve, Pop and Grandma Biddie Kells made a little fest for all his kids—Dad, his brothers, sisters, and their kids.

Pop Kells bought a bunch of candles at Big Bob's Liquidating and it was the perfect night. It was beautiful. Dad's brothers and sisters and Dad and mom left about 7:30 for their next stops. My mom and dad's next stop every year was Pop and Nana Trosk's. On Cummisky Street. Their house is shown below:

Pop Trosk loved Breezie in a different way than Pop Kells. Breezie spent every day when mom and dad had gone to work for years at Pop Kells house. Both pops loved the doggie to pieces. Pop Trosk every year bought Breezie three squeak toys and placed them with all the gifts under the Trosk tree.

He also put up a little platform up with an HO gauge train and he ran it for everybody before they had the gift opening. Here is his train and tree.

Each year, Pop Trosk offered everybody a little schnorkie right before he sang Silent Night. He did it well. His eyes always filled up near the end of his singing.

By the time he finished all of his adult children and Mom were crying. Dad admits to wetting up a bit on Christmas Eve at the Trosks also.

This year, Pop Trosk had a new friend, our new puppy, Breezie who after Silent Night, seemed to know it would be a good night for him. It was.

Mom's brothers and sisters were a bit taken back when Pop Trosk called Breezie first to go find his gifts that Pop had wrapped for him. It was not the way it had ever been for the Trosk siblings before Breezie.

Breezie did not miss one of the three items that Pop had carefully wrapped and placed around the tree. He found them all. Mom's brothers and sisters were sure he would grab one of their gifts by mistake, but he did not.

He plowed through all the other stacked gifts but did not break anything. One by one he brought each little gift of his into a small clearing on the floor where nobody was sitting and there had been no other gifts.

With a clever combination of his teeth and his paws, he unwrapped each gift, one by one. Each was a different shaped squeak toy. He made no mistakes. The siblings and mom and dad were in awe. Breezie eventually won all the Trosks siblings over. From then on, they trusted him.

Once he was able to squeak the toy, Breezie went back again for the next and the next, repeating his unwrapping ritual each time.

By the third unwrapping of the third squeak toy, the Trosk siblings had confidence that Breezie would pick only his own gifts and they too were able to enjoy his antics as much as mom and dad and Pot Trosk and Nana Trosk. It was a magical night.

When Pop ran the HO train, it made it even more magical.

Mom and dad have often talked about how wonderful Christmas Eve was up at the Trosk homestead with kielbasa, smoked and fresh, and Eggnog and the schnorkies and other great cheer. What a gift if today we could go back and relive something like that.

Moving next door

In March, 1976, mom and dad and Breezie moved into their new digs on 47 Perfect Street after living in Apartment 2 on 49 Perfect Street for about four or five months. It was all done. Pop Kells did a great job.

Dad had some great friends such as Denny Bucko Grimes, Joshy and Georgie Bohunk, Geraldo Tobe, Frannys Xavier Kurilla, Mikey Kurilla, and others.

Uncle Joe and Uncle Ed were always willing to help dad and he helped them when needed.

The great crew of nephews and nieces in the Kelly family all showed up for the move to the eight rooms next door from the apartment and the move was finished in just one day.

Besides the humans, there was other help. For example, there was a quarter of Erlanger Beer, dad's favorite at the time, and a pot of Mom's Chile Con Carne.

As usual, all of the Abe's hotdogs, the Chile, and every drop of Erlanger Beer kicked as the timing was as perfect as the name, Perfect Street.

Though everybody was tired, there was some other beer left over from someplace. Dad is not sure when the keg kicked if what he found was cans or bottles or both. We as a family were not on E (empty).

Relaxing after the move, mom and dad sat at the new kitchen table and Mom decided she needed some chocolate. She had a frozen rabbit that she had recently moved to the new refrigerator.

The guy who had originally carried that refrigerator and freezer up the front steps and into the house was sitting right in front of the Fridge.

While enjoying one of the last beers in the whole house, he was accosted by a chocolate rabbit while Mom was fetching it from the freezer.

You see, as mom tried to grab the rabbit, it was a bit icy and it slipped out of her hands and smashed big Franny Kurilla, a gentle giant, in the nose and lip. Some of dad's friends were saying he had carried in the refrigerator with one hand.

Most of dad's buddies had seen Franny rip huge doors off big buildings for less provocation than a cut lip and bruised nose. .

There was silence until a nose-bleeding Franny Kurilla laughed and laughed and laughed. Then, he too enjoyed the chocolate and beer along with his beautiful wife Joanne, who he loved profusely.

He and she laughed harder than anybody according to dad. What a great day they all had. What a great hand they had lent to mom and dad to accomplish the move. Life was just beginning for mom and dad Kells.

Chapter 5 Life on 47 Perfect Street

So, mom and dad were now in the big house. Looking on from the front, it was the right side of the double block—all eight rooms. Pop Kells had it all polished up.

In the stories my parents told, I learned that mom and dad felt that it did not take them long to adjust to the eight rooms on the right side of the big white house on 47 Perfect Street. It was perfect.

While they were getting accustomed to their new life on the big side of the block on Perfect Street, Pop Kells built one more thing for them.

He and dad got some porch-wood from a lumber yard and Pop Kells built a big beautiful bar in what our family called the family room. It was the third room from the front of the house downstairs, right next to the kitchen. Others called it the gold room.

Dad loved buying carpet remnants from Giant Floor. He picked up a beautiful brown patterned rug for the family room. It was about one foot short on all four sides. So dad found this rust colored expensive carpeting. They only had a few pieces and they were small and cheap. It was just enough.

Dad put the patterned rug in the middle of the floor and then cut the solid rust colored rug to go around it. It actually looked like a picture in a frame on the floor. I must say that it was very nice. It must have been very durable carpet.

Thirteen years later when the family moved to South Wilkes-Barre, that carpeting still looked like new. The family room was where we spent most of our time on Perfect Street so that says a lot.

Dad tells me that about ten years after that when mom and dad finally sold 47-49 Perfect Street, that the twenty-three-year-old carpeting in the family room was the same and it still looked sharp. Nice job Dad!

BTW, Pop Kells painted all the walls gold in that room except the wall with the brick paneling. I had forgotten about that.

All the while I lived there, the walls were gold but the brick paneled wall opposite the kitchen looked like real bricks. The built-in bar that Pop Kells built from scratch out of porch-wood, was the center of attention.

During the construction of the brick paneling in that room, dad tells a great story about Pop Kells, my grandpop. Dad bought Pop four home remodeling books (a great set that was not cheap) for his retirement. Pop received them graciously but never seemed to be reading them.

When Pop Kells was doing the brick-like paneling, however, he cheered up his middle child, my dad. He told dad that he made good use of the books.

He said that the 8-foot paneling was about one inch short of where he wanted it to lay and the four one-inch thick books helped him boost the paneling up to where he wanted to have it for easy nailing.

Dad got a kick out of it, but my guess is that secretly Dad had hoped Pop would have found some secret techniques for construction rather than having used the books to prop up the paneling. Just saying!

Coming in the front door of the new living quarters, on the left was a hallway that took you right to the open stairway which led to the second of two floors. Here is a picture of dad showing off at Christmas time on the beautiful open stairway.

To the right of the open stairway at the end of the front hallway was the dining room. Mom bought a nice tropical looking green rug, and with the wall paper, it dad a definite tropical look.

On the next page, you can see the dining room wall-paper with Christmas stockings and gifts galore.

The other walls were painted white. After pop painted the other walls, dad did the papering such as the tropical look in this dining room.

After that, moving towards the back of the house was a door that was always open. Going through, you would be in the family room (always gold with the bar and the brick paneling).

I can still see the beauty of this room as we all watched TV here and we would hook up special computers to the big TV (for the times) so everybody could see the games and the contests.

To the left of that door opening, under the steps was another door to a large closet. Moving towards the back again, on the left side of the wall that had the brick look, was the kitchen door.

I do not ever remember it closed so I conclude that it was also always open. Before you would get into the kitchen, there was a very short hallway and on the right was the cellar door.

The cellar steps were immediately under the back steps that would take us upstairs. The back steps entrance was on the right side of the kitchen.

If we chose not to go up the back steps, then straight through the kitchen from the inside family room door was the back door. It opened to the outside onto a deck and the back yard.

We made a lot of use of that back deck and dad eventually connected the porch deck to the swimming pool deck, which you can see in the next picture.

Mikey and I in 1982, are shown on the pool deck that was connected to the porch deck. I'll tell you about all that soon.

If you could see to the right, it was the spot where this lower deck met the pool seats and where those who wanted to swim simply jumped in. I could not find pictures of the pool but this gives the idea. Right after the picture of Mike and I is a Muskin pool like ours.

Picture Mikey and I on the inside of the wooden deck on the left below:

OK folks, it is time to get out of the pool.

Moving back to the small living room to the right as you first walked into the house, it has a magical Christmas story to tell all on its own. This room was about 11' X 12'.

We had lived from March, 1976, in the eight rooms on this side of the block and by now, mom and dad were quite accustomed to it. Before Christmas after the first anniversary on Perfect Street, Dad had begun to make some holiday purchases.

He first bought a 5X9 platform with 18 inch legs. He said it was like the platform he had on High Street where he lived as a kid. I was not born yet, but I loved dad telling this story.

Dad put the platform up well before Christmas and then with his checkbook in his hand, with mom by his side, Dad went to Frank's Roundhouse about a month before Christmas, 1975, and he bought a big LGB train.

It was a starter train without a caboose. It looked like an overstuffed HO Train but it was twice the size of a Lionel. Everything looked big.

There were only two tracks like HO but they were about twice a wide as the three-track Lionel's. The picture on the next page is how it looked on the shelf at Frank's Roundhouse.

Frank Rash owned the place and he had been dad's high school baseball coach. So, we got a good deal. Later, six years after I was born, I played T-Ball for Mr. Rash's team at St. Theresa's Little League. As you might expect, our team name was Frank's RoundHouse. Frank Rash had sponsored the team.

As we discussed in the last chapter, Pop Trosk always put up a nice HO train on Cummiskey Street during the holidays and I always liked that as a kid. Dad's train was huge compared to that.

Dad said he put the two 4'X5' platforms together and bolted the eight 18" legs onto the corners. The combined platform size was 8' X 5".

Dad had figured that the big curve on the LGB needed five feet so a 4X8 standard platform would not go. And so from left to right there was curved track then straight track met a matching curved set of tracks from the other side, coming together in an oval. It was another part of the magical about living on Perfect Street.

When I was born four years later, dad was still creating the platform every year and it was a thing of beauty just like it was the first year. I saw the pictures.

Dad always put this green paper on the platform before he put the track down. It was coated with a picky grass like substance and when the platform was in full bloom, it looked like a field of green grass. Mom always added a few pretty houses and stuff like that.

I saw it on the pictures that mom and dad kept from their first Christmas in the big house. The tree was placed on the left side on one of the 4X5 bolted pieces and on the other side was the yard which was sometimes green and sometimes snowy. It changed from year to year.

Dad said that shortly after he moved to the big house, he and Uncle Joe and Uncle Ed began to play darts with Pop Kells at the Wilkes-Barre Republic Club.

Dad's mom, whom we all called Grandma Biddie because Pop Kells called her Biddie, would come up to our house to spend time with mommy and Breezie when dad and Pop Kells went to play darts. Mom loved that and so did dad. Breezie loved Grandmom Kells the most.

They told me a lot of stories about the early days before I was born. I loved listening to them.

Chapter 6 The Stork Brings Me to Perfect Street

It was about five and a half years after Mom and Dad were married that God gave the Stork specific instructions as to where to deliver me. It was May 28, 1980 but I remember nothing about it.

He delivered me to Mercy Hospital in Wilkes-Barre but shortly afterwards, mom and dad took me to our Perfect Street home. e

The full story that I was told was that Mom had a long labor of almost 24 hours and I finally came through the window of my mom's hospital room in early evening on May 28. Dad and mom were thrilled, as they have told me many times.

They did not forget to tell me that there were stork feathers on the hospital floor.

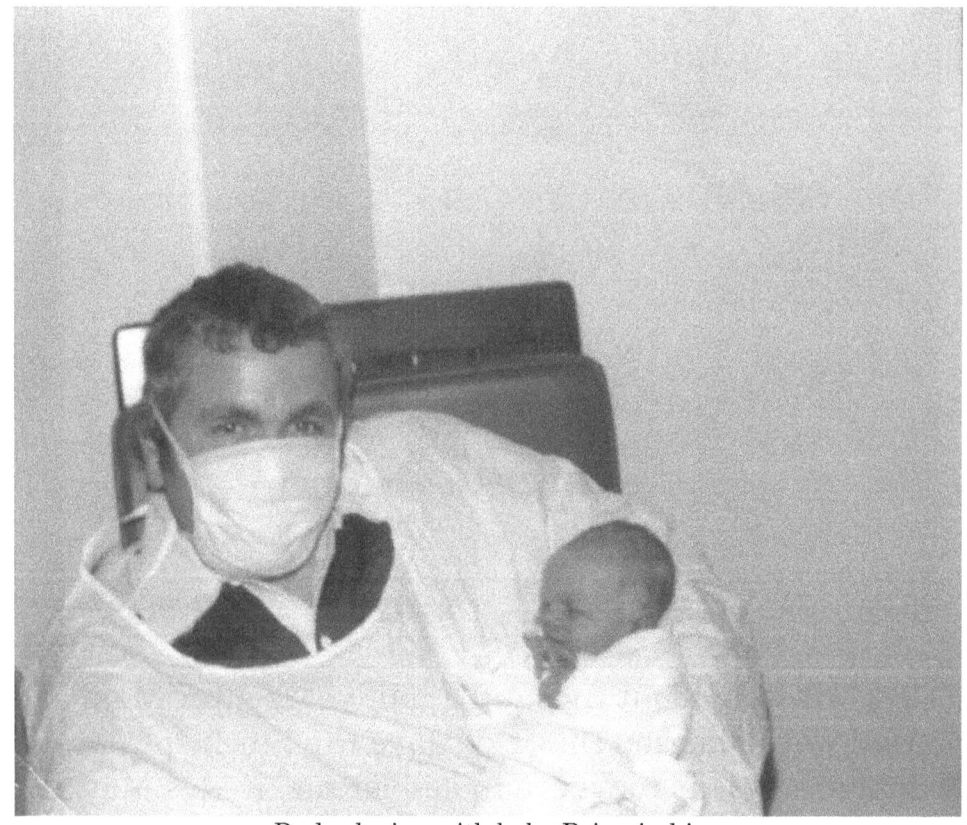

Dad relaxing with baby Brian in his arms

Everything went well with me, thankfully. Dr. Horan literally showed dad he had a little boy and he had dad do his duty with something called the umbilical cord. Dr. John Rogers, who dad played baseball with at King's College did the in-hospital operation, so I could go home. After a few days, it was time to head for Perfect Street.

All the while at the hospital, the two pops and the two nanas were visiting and there were nurses taking care of me when mom was sleeping (not much sleep she says.) I was never alone it seemed. Dad and mom always had lots of help they say, in the hospital.

Dad pulled the car up to the hospital door. Mom was already there with me all bundled up. They brought us down in a wheel chair for safety. It was late morning and not very hot yet for May 28. Dad already had a baby car seat in the back and that is where they put me right next to mom. But first, they took a picture of mom holding me in the front seat before we took off on our way home:

Mom and Baby Brian in the car for this picture

The parking spot in front of the house on Perfect Street was open so dad parked right there. Our door was on the sidewalk side.

Mom and Brian on Perfect Street

Dad came around and opened the door and mom got me out of the seat constraints. She carried me up the eight steps to the front door on 47 Perfect Street. Dad trailed behind in case if anything went wrong, he could catch us. Dad then passed us and opened the door.

As we went in dad said he felt alone and somewhat scared as he and mom were bringing a real live baby into the house for the first time. Mom and dad looked at each other and their looks said, "now what?"

There were no pops or nanas there to make it all OK for my parents this time. They said they immediately felt the responsibility to make sure I was OK.

By the end of the day, the pops and the nanas and a number of relatives and friends had stopped in to see the new baby. It was me.

My white crib, which we got from Mr. Plescik, Big Franny's wife's dad, was all set up and before long, mom said, I was in my crib and sound asleep giving the new parents a short break.

Because as they told me, I had my nights and day's mixed up, it would be a long time before mom and dad got any real rest again.

I took a lot of mom and dad's time in the early days. As I said, I had my nights and days mixed up. I apparently did not like it at all when mom and dad were asleep.

On the next page is a picture of me and mom and dad and our wonderful dog Breezie right after we got home.

This picture was taken in our dining room on Perfect Street. Notice the tropical wallpaper that mom had selected for the back wall.

Mr. Trosk, who was aka grandpop Trosk, but who I eventually called Pop Trosk, never liked to use his real first name. He preferred the name *Smoke or Smokey* instead of Stanley. All the kids called him Grand Pop or Pop Trosk.

I always wondered whether he smoked a lot or he like smoked kielbasa, which he always served on the major holidays. Regardless, *the Smoke* liked me and I knew it.

The next big event that started on Perfect Street was my Christening. Below are a bunch of pictures from that great day. The priest who baptized me was Father John Terry. He also baptized my brother Mikey and sister Katie.

His father, Mr. Buddy Terry worked with my father at IBM in Scranton. He is a wonderful priest. Here is a picture of me and mom getting ready for my baptism.

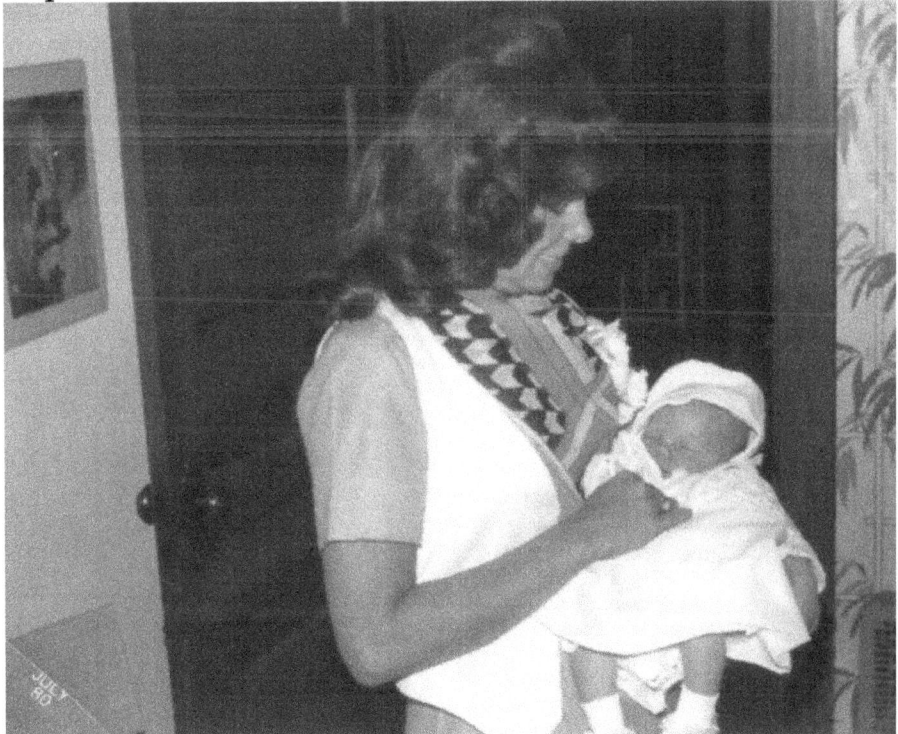

On the next page is a nice picture of me and mom and nana Trosk who was helping mom get me ready for the Christening:

Below is Father John Terry at the Christening with my Godmother Aunt Sue and Aunt Cathy and Dad.

When the Christening was over, we all went back to Perfect Street for the party. Here is a picture of me with my Godmother Aunt Sue and Godfather, Uncle Joe and a bunch of my uncles and aunts at the front of St. Patrick's church as we were leaving the Christening. See Aunt Hey Hey and he mom Carrie in the front:

And, that was that. The regular living began the next day.

In April 1980, dad bought an 18-foot round pool right from the Muskin company where Mr. Mike Kurilla and his buddy Mr. Romy Shedleski both worked. The Kurilla's lived downstairs on 49 Perfect Street and the

Evans,' Karen and Ken, lived upstairs. Mr. Kurilla and Mr. Shedleski got dad a great deal on the pool.

Better than that, they both knew how to install Muskin above-ground pools and they had our pool up and running in about a week. Everybody helped to install the pool.

By the time I got home in May, the pool was up and running and my cousins, the Dales and the Flannerys had already had a few swims in the new pool.

Being only a week or so old, I was unaware that year that we had a pool, but I have been told that I was always around all the pool action. I first spotted the new Muskin Pool after Dad opened it in late May 1980, I was in wonderment. Dad had it ready to go earlier but the water was too cold for anybody.

Memorial Day was the first warm day. It was on May 26, two days before I was born. The Dales and the Flannery's (my Aunt Nancy's crew) had already tried out the new pool. Dad told me the pool water was quite cold before the holiday, but by Memorial day, it was warm enough to swim.

There were always squirrels by the big trees in our back yard. Sometimes they would be on the seats on the top of the pool until dad would chase them. Before long all the kids were singing a song dad made up.

They would sing it when they would make a whirl pool to help clean up any debris that was in the pool.

After the whirl pool, the leaves, etc., would all be in a little pile in the middle of the pool.

Dad would get the kids singing:

This is not a squirrel pool
This is a whirl-pool.

Go ahead sing it and repeat it until enough is enough. It was so much fun, my brother and sister and everybody else sang it for years.

Before the summer was over, two of the three Bee kids, David and Kimmee, from next door would come to swim as did the Callahans. Mr. Bee and Mrs. Bee came too and they would swim to cool off. Here is a picture of Nana Trosk on the back deck with me in July 1980:

Dad told me that all summer long when mom was outside with everybody and dad was at work at IBM, she kept me mostly in my "baby seat" next door with the back door open. The door was just to the left of the picture above with Nana Trosk.

When you would go into the back entrance of 47 Perfect Street, there was a miniature foyer. That's where mom kept me most of the time, out of the sun and safe from the porch and pool traffic On the right side was the door to the first-floor apartment and straight ahead was the door to the second-floor apartment which was basically a set of steps. It was my shade nook.

Thanksgiving & The 1980 Christmas Season

In 1980 when I was a baby, Mom said that it was great having company all summer, but it was an awful lot of work. By the time Thanksgiving came, I had taken so many pictures with my eyes that I was starting to make sense out of some things in life, or so I thought. I was six months old at Thanksgiving.

I was crawling wherever I needed to go. Mom and dad put a big gate at the top of the front inside steps so I would not fall down the steps. They also put cushions on all the sharp table corners to protect my eyes when I was in my walker. There even covers on the electrical outlets.

From right before Thanksgiving, mom was decorating the house for Christmas.

Dad had an IBM computer account in Millville, PA called Girton Manufacturing. He invited our great friends the Komorek's, Al and Karen to go to Millville with him and mom to get a nice fresh-cut tree. They agreed.

Nana and Pop watched me while my parents went for the fresh cut tree.

Mom and dad always talked about what great trips they were. After picking the pre-cut tree in the Guzmar's front yard in Millville, PA, they would put the tree inside the VW Bus and head off to the Motel McGee in Bloomsburg.

It was dinner at Dick Benefield's Groaning Board. They bragged about the super smorgasbord that accompanied the great dinner. One year, Al Harding from Girton Manufacturing in Millville joined mom and dad for dinner.

When dad and mom got home, dad put the tree in the house and the very next day, he set up the platform with the green paper already on it from years before.

The first year that he had put up the platform and train, dad had laid the track down and made sure the split for the two platforms was right where the back and front tracks separated.

He had tacked it down so they track would stay in place even after the two sides were separated. That way, he had a lot of work already done for the following years like this one. So, this time, when he set up the platform, he simply joined the tracks from the two 4X5 pieces and created the big 5X8 platform.

Mom had me in my baby seat as Dad put the engine on the track and connected the lock-on to the transformer. He made sure that the train would travel smoothly across all the tracks—curved and straight.

It was great. I can almost remember seeing it all happen as mom watched me while dad ran the train engine for the first time to make sure it was OK. It was fine.

Dad then then put the tree in the fresh tree holder and moved the tree and holder onto the left side of the platform. To make sure the tree would not fall, dad put two nails in the wall and he wrapped wires around the tree and then wrapped the wires around the nails. The way dad set it up, the tree was not going anywhere.

Mom always offered dad advice about how to do everything. When dad tried to put another car on the train, mom said not to do that until all the lights and ornaments were on the tree as she would have to walk on the platform to get that job done.

Dad weighed over 200 pounds then. Today he is over 300 pounds but to me, he still looks good. He actually looks like Santa Claus and his big belly makes it even more so.

He found the beams where the wood was in the platform and with mom on the floor, dad started at the top of the tree and he put all the lights on the tree.

They all worked. Then dad got the white garland and put it around the tree. He bought a pack of icicles but mom did not want them on with the garland, so dad said OK.

Mom then got out the old ornaments from their time in the apartment and the new ones she had just bought over the years. She carefully put them all on the tree and she saved the newest ornament, "Baby's First Christmas" as the last ornament.

When she had the tree decorated and it was all beautiful and sparkly, she called dad over and gave him a kiss. They shared some wine together before mom announced that it was time to put the top on the tree.

I don't know what the top looked like as mom would often get a new top each Christmas. I know it had electric wires, so dad had to get back up on the platform and find where he could plug it in.

When he got it plugged in and it was all lit, he reached up very carefully and set it on the very top of the tree. Mom guided him to get it straight and he did a great job according to mom. The tree was done.

Dad bought some mountain paper this year and he put a couple boxes together on the left side of the tree and a bit in the back.

He cut holes in the boxes so that they would form the basis for the holes in the tunnel he was building. I have pictures of this, but I can't find any with the mountains he built that year.

Dad put the boxes where he wanted them and then he ran the engine again to make sure that it would fit going inside and then out of the tunnel. It all worked. Rather than remove the boxes, dad tacked them down and put on the mountain paper carefully.

Here is a picture of a pre-made LGB tunnel. The one dad made was much more realistic:

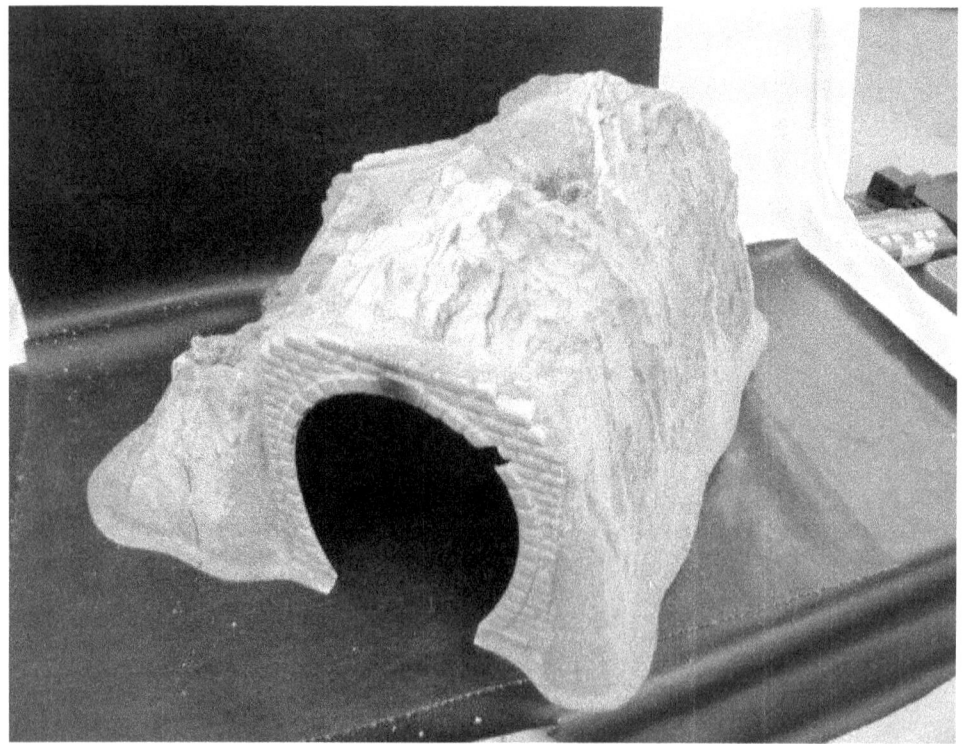

Dad used some Scotch Tape and some tacks to make sure the pieces of mountain paper after being wrinkled to give it the mountain look would stay in place. It took about a half hour as they told me because it was a delicate job. That big tunnel was wonderful.

I may not have seen it well when I was six months old but every year after, dad would do the same thing. Then, one year from being stored in the cellar, the tunnel mostly fell apart and the tree did the job of the tunnel from then on.

We used Four gifts from God (above) pretending they are were platform decorations. From left to right is my best buddy Dawn, Katie, Me, and then Mikey.

You can see in the picture shown on the prior page from Christmas in 1987, that after we had moved to our new house. Dad used the same tree and train platform.

As the years went by, my brother Mikey and my sister Kate and I loved the train platform and the train. I called it the Toot Toot, and Mike and Katie called it the Choo-Choo Woo-Woo!

Back in December 1980, when dad was done building the mountain and the tunnel for the train platform, he turned it over to mom.

She was waiting to begin the delicate work of setting up houses, the ice-skating rink, the roads, the people including the carolers, and the streetlights and anything else mom thought was needed.

Mom put snow from a box they bought on the entire left side of the platform. She covered the sides of the ice-skating rink with snow too and added the ice-skaters. She put Santa's workshop there and a gingerbread house. You can see them in the picture.

They were close to the tree, which had its own snow covering via a white tree blanket. It was beautiful. You could hardly tell that the green paper was underneath it all—until you looked to the right side of the platform.

Here is where mom's artistic talents came in. She and dad had bought about ten houses and a church and a railway station. Mom used old coffee grounds and created roads.

She put the church in the middle of the village and put the train station in the front. She put the houses right by the roads, so they looked perfect. She then added some people walking and some cars on the roads and some street lamps.

This first year of my life, the street lamps did not light nor did the houses but as time went by in the following years, mom figured out how to light up the houses and the street lights. It was spectacular.

When the platform homes etc. were all in place, mom asked dad to put the train on the tracks. We had an engine, a tender (where they kept the coal), a cattle car, and a flat bed. After this was the caboose.

Dad got it all together and then said that it was time for her first spin. The engine had a light and it worked as did all the other lights. The train zoomed around the platform and then hit the mountain and the tunnel, and it all disappeared for an instant.

We saw the light on the other side of the tunnel and soon the train and all the cars were out of the tunnel heading for another run around the platform. It was great. Mom and dad were thrilled and they said that when I looked at it all, I had a little twinkle in my eye.

There were just two more things to do.

Dad bought a skirt for the platform that was made of cardboard. It was a red-brick-looking skirt that covered up the under side of the 18" high platform. When dad got that finished with thumbtacks to hold it on, there was just one more thing to do.

Just that day, dad came home with a nice white wooden fence that was about five inches high. He put the fence up on every area of the outside top of the platform wherever there was no wall.

Dad set the fireplace paper so there was a little slit where the wires from the transformer went up to the track. You could not see the wires or the transformer until dad chose to bring the transformer out from under the platform. It was clever. Wow! What a beautiful job dad!.

Mom said after all that work setting up the tree and platform in 1980, we were ready for Christmas. She said the beautiful fresh tree from Millville was perfectly shaped and it smelled great.

On Christmas day, I can sort of recall a pile of wrapped items sitting right next to that fireplace paper with the platform and tree in the background. There was a tree, and when I opened up my presents that year, there were toys, and of course on Christmas Eve and Christmas day, there was the big Toot-Toot buzzing around the platform. It was peeking in and out of the mountain and around the big tree. You bet it was magical. Mom and dad loved their first Christmas with their first little man.

Chapter 7 Baby Brian's First Christmas--1980

We had the tree up weeks before Christmas eve. On Christmas Eve, mom and dad drove me to St. Patrick's Church about a mile away for 4:30 Mass. Dad and the two Pops, Uncle Joe, and Uncle Ed had been at the Republic Club before that for their afternoon free-open house. Right after church we drove to meet my Kells cousins for Christmas at Pop Kells' house.

I was in the back in the baby-seat because we first went to church and right after the Kells celebration, we were heading up Pop Trosks.

In the picture above, Pop Kells was taking a breather on Christmas Eve.

I don't remember much but Pop Kells had a nice house and a nice tree, and it smelled good in the house. It was crowded with lots of kids and the uncles and aunts. Everybody had already eaten by the time we got there as St. Pat's Mass was always a little late.

Before anybody opened any presents, Grandma Biddie came into the living room and faced the tree. Pop Kells announced that she was going to finish decorating Pop's tree.

Grandma Biddie (her real name is Irene) had something white and shiny behind her back and when she got to the tree, like a baseball player, she wound up and threw it on the tree. It was angel hair and it landed about a foot from the top of the tree. It was beautiful where it was so nobody moved it. Here is what it looked like:

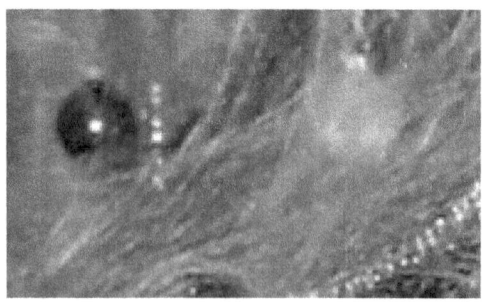

Everybody cheered and clapped and then mom picked me up and grabbed a seat for the two of us for the gift openings.

Everybody loved it as all the gifts were given out. and I can kinda remember I loved it too. Mom had a little pile for me and I can recall there were a lot of shiny things in my pile.

From there, we went back in the car. Mom and dad had stuff from Pop Kells and stuff for her brothers & sisters, & mom and dad at Pop Trosk's house.

I forgot to say before that Breezie, our dog was with us at Pop Kells. Even though we did not eat, the dog ate a lot. Breezie and mom were in the back seat with me when we went to Pop Trosks.

When we got to the Trosks it took dad two or more trips to get all the stuff for the Trosk house up their steps and inside through the front door. It was not long that all my uncles and aunts and Aunt Cathy Piotroski and my Trosk cousins, Marty, Scott, Erin, and Justin were all there. Starting with Pop and Nana, here are a few pictures from that night:

They all came and it was not long before we were all there. Pop had the tree and the HO train set up. Dad was holding Breezie as nobody wanted him to root for his gifts before they were ready to celebrate.

The Marty Trosk Family in Nana Trosk's Kitchen

We all had some refreshments and some Kielbasa from Swantkos in Nanticoke, I had my little sippy cup and mom made sure I was OK. I was the youngest one there, including Breezie.

Pop passed out schnorkies, gave his toast, and sang Silent night. As always, he was weeping as were many adults when he finished. Then he ran the train.

Breezie was getting fidgety when Pop Trosk ran the train.

Then Trosk Pop called Breezie and just like the year before, he found his three squeak toys and everybody began to call out names and eventually everybody had their gifts in front of them.

Breezie was in the corner with his three squeak toys loving every minute of the Christmas celebration. Every now and then Pop Trosk would slip Breezie a piece of Kielbasa. They had fresh and smoked varieties.

Everybody was enjoying the gifts they got as were Pop and Nana (Arline) Trosk. Mom opened my gifts with me and I remember there were toys and they seemed all shiny. It was nice.

Eventually it was time to go.

When we got back to Perfect Street, mom said she told me all about Santa and that good things would happen over-night when Santa came. Dad and mom tucked me in and I fell right asleep for the whole night.

I guess I should say that I had visions of sugar plums dancing in my head but I am not sure that I did. I do know that it was such a nice night that I smiled all the while.

That morning before I knew what was going on, Dad had me in his arms. He changed me (We don't have to talk about that) and he brought me downstairs. Mom had a camera and got a lot of great pictures. Mom told me the story of this, my first Christmas, many times since. I was a lucky baby.

Dad put me down on the living room rug right by a pile of gifts. Mom kept snapping pictures. In the pictures that I remember I was in the middle of all the gifts.

Here is a picture of Dad on Christmas day coming down the open staircase.

To mom and dad, they told me I was their best gift ever. Of course, that was before Mikey and Katie showed up over the next several years.

All gifts this first Christmas appeared to be toys and they were all shiny and happy looking. I wish I could remember what they were.

Though I do not recall getting it on Christmas day, I do know that year I got a magnetic blackboard and a couple sets of letters and numbers that would stick to the board. Throughout the year of 1981 and even 1982, I played with that board all the time.

Mom said that before too long, because dad and Pop Trosk were always showing me numbers and letters, I began to count early and I was able to form small words like dog and cat. I remember loving stuff like that.

After we opened all of my gifts, mom said I noticed two more piles by the tree. They were from mom to dad and from dad to mom. We left them there and I did not complain.

Mom then picked me up and walked me three rooms hence and put me in the high chair in the kitchen for my Christmas breakfast. I am sure it was some great Gerber product, which I had all the time and which I recall I loved very much. I was about seven months old at the time.

Mom and dad carried me down to Pop Kells and Grandma Biddie's house for Christmas dinner a little after noon. They lived about six doors down from us. We had a nice Turkey Dinner with Pop Kells and Grandma Biddie. Breezie always got his share from Biddie.

We stayed awhile watching football and then we walked back home, and mom told me I was tired so she put me up for an afternoon nap in my crib. The crib was in the pink room, which four years later became my sister Kate's room.

Dad still had his office in the room next door tomy room. I think mom and dad took a nap as they too were tuckered out from the night before.

In addition to Pop and Grandma Biddie, Pop and Nana Trosk always had a big Turkey dinner for Christmas day. Even Breezie was tired so he slept on the cool kitchen floor. Mom got me up and got me all dressed up again for Christmas at the Trosks.

Pop Trosk was watching football and Dad joined him in the living room. Nana set up the dining-room which did not happen often. When Nana called everybody to eat, the Trosks all found seats at the big table. Mom and I were with them.

Pop Trosk and dad ate dinner in the kitchen. Pop Trosk had come in from visiting friends at the Legion. Dad really loved being with Pop Trosk. Everybody had a great time and the turkey was absolutely delicious.

Because there were giblets in the gravy, Dad had an extra wad of potatoes instead of stuffing. Dad was never a giblet guy.

When Grandma Biddie passed away, we began to make dinner ourselves for Thanksgiving and Christmas, Dad always boiled the giblets for Breezie and the dog smacked his lips as he consumed every morsel.

Because Christmas Eve had been such a late night this year, everybody was tired. Santa was good to everybody as I recall mom saying. It was now very dark. We left the Trosks with another pile of gifts that we had left behind the night before. .

When we got home, mom and dad tucked me in almost right away, I went right to sleep. Mom said there was a ton of food in the house and dad said that he gained at least five pounds over the holidays.

I remember them taking me to a lot of houses over the holidays. Nana and Pop Trosk came down the house and Pop Kells and Grandma Biddie joined us to bring in the new year.

A next door lady on the other side of the Tudor Double block, Kaye Pavlick, came over and joined us all. Barbara and Joseph Bee were also there. We played Guy Lombardo music and had some champagne. Mom still loves champagne.

We called Mrs. Pavlov Good Kaye because she was a good lady and it sounded good. On New Year's Eve, . the two pops and nanas, mom and dad, and Good Kaye danced in the gold room and when somebody spinned Good Kaye, she always went *whee!*

It was a great New Years' Eve. It was next a great New Years' Day. Mom said that Dad watched every bowl game there was on New Years' Day while most of the time I was napping. Mom took care of me that day and every day.

It was January 1, 1981. This was my first holiday of my second calendar year alive. I was about to learn that there were a lot of other holidays and a great summer in which to look forward. I did.

Chapter 8 St. Patrick's Day and Easter 1981

I was soon talking and walking

St. Patrick's Day came like clockwork, two and a half months after New Year's Day. It was what mom called, another cold winter. Dad was away for several weeks as he liked to get his IBM technical education classes out of the way early in the year. He had classes in Texas and in Rochester, Minnesota.

By St. Patrick's Day, the weather had warmed up quite a bit. On Saturday, March 14, 1981, Wilkes-Barre City held their annual St. Patrick's Day Parade.

Mom and Dad parked in the Station Parking Lot and pushed my stroller to South Main Street to see the parade. It was great. We had a wonderful view of all the great action.

They had dressed me warm so I felt very good and every now and then somebody would throw some soft candy, which my parents would swoop up and give me a taste.

They had everything in this parade. I had never heard or seen bagpipers, but they filled the streets of Wilkes-Barre on this Saturday afternoon for the city's second annual St. Patrick's Day Parade. The most recent parade in 2018 was the 38th.

There were dozens of floats and marching bands from all the schools and a place called The Irem Temple. They all entertained the crowd, including me, and mom and dad and there were about 500 participants and perhaps more in this great event. I was amazed at the huge Fire Engines. It was my first parade.

Mom and dad took me, and Michael and Katie to many such parades, including the Santa Claus parade at Christmas time.

It seemed like just an instant and we were back in the car headed home. Dad made a combination of corned beef brisket and ham and cabbage and potatoes and we enjoyed that meal on Sunday. Dad still makes a great St. Patrick's day dinner plus he buys about five dinners at St. Patrick's Church.

The next big family holiday was on Easter. Pop Kelly had a big chicken dinner on Easter in which all the Kelly's were invited including me. Pop Trosk had a similar dinner which we attended.

Most often Uncle Marty and Aunt Cathy and Marty, Erin, and Scott were the only Trosks who made it besides mom and dad. After dinner for over fifty years now, my mom put on a very nice Easter Egg hunt.

Yes, from when she was eighteen years old and little Marty Trosk was just born, mom ran an Easter Egg hunt. It was always in Pop Trosk's big yard on Cummiskey Street in Wilkes-Barre.

This year was no different. Pop Kelly and all the Kelly cousins who were born all come to the hunt. It kept getting bigger. I was eleven months old and could walk by then, but I still needed dad to help me collect my bag of eggs.

Mom also walked with me in my first Easter Egg Hunt and I found over twenty aluminum wrapped chocolate Easter Eggs. The Easter Bunny had wrapped them tight.

Everybody loved it. Mom gave the winner a really big bunny. I forget who won the event in my first Easter Egg hunt but I can remember we all loved it. What a great time for kids. It sure looked like the adults were having fun also.

Chapter 9 The Summer of 1981

This was dad's first year in which he had to get the Muskin pool set up for the summer without Mike Kurilla and Romy Shedleski being there for him.

Both the Mike Kurilla Family and the Ken Evans family were still living in the apartments, so he had any help that he needed right in our building. But, he got it done himself.

Dad said it was lots easier than he had thought. He first took off the cover and unfortunately, it had developed a hole over the winter so the dirty water and the leaves on the top of the cover seeped into the pool.

Dad had brought the pool level down below the skimmer in the fall when he put on the cover. This was to make sure the plastic skimmer would not freeze during the winter and then bust.

So, his first step was to hook up the pool pump and the sand filter again to keep the water in the pool. Then he began to fill the pool with the hose.

In about eight hours, the pool was high enough that dad could turn on the pump. When he did, everything worked. But, the water was very dirty.

The next thing dad did was to get the leaf skimmers attached to the handles so he and mom could work on getting the wet, rotting leaves out.

When that was done, dad set the filter to waste and while the hose was putting water in, the murky water that was taken from the bottom was spilling out onto the ground. After that the pool was pretty clear. Dad refilled it about a foot a few times to keep the dirty water elimination going..

Dad brought the water level up, added a little sand to the filter, and then he ran the pump, backwashing periodically. Each day for two to three days, it kept getting more clear.

In three days it was ready for swimmers, But it was just the second week in May and it was still too cold.

Something great happened in the Spring time. My new buddy Dawn, who was my age, moved in next door with her brother Dave and her sister Kim. Mr. Joseph Bee and Barbara Bee moved their family next door to us from Grove Street. They were great.

I got to know the Bees first and we liked them all. When Mikey was born and about a year old in 1983, Mr. Bee took a real liking to him and he helped him learn to swim.

I was with all the Bee kids the first warm day of 1981 around Memorial day. Nobody knew how to swim.

Mom was in the pool with me on my first day. She had me in a little ducky inner-tube and she had inflatable arms that were called swimmies at the time.

It did not take long for me to be able to navigate the pool without mom holding on. By the end of May, I was a whole one-year old.

Despite how good I got, all summer long, mom never let me in the pool by myself. Looking back, I understand why.

Dave and Kim were tall enough that they could stand on their toes and be out of the water. Dawn was little like me. She too needed the tube & the swimmies.

The Bees had an old pool in their yard that was not in good shape. The Zims formerly lived there and Dad said they did not use the pool much. The Bee kids, Mr. Bee, and Barbie Bee were in our pool more than we were, so they got rid of their old pool.

I remember that it looked unusable anyway. There was no patching it. Mr. Bee had to dismantle it piece by piece. It took a few weeks before it was gone.

When he had all the metal from the pool in one place, he put it in his trunk and sold it to Solomon's Junk Yard a few blocks away for a few bucks.

With the money he got, he bought some nectar and he made a great fondue for everybody to enjoy. Our families often celebrated with nectar together. Dad made sure that Mr. Bee knew that he could use our pool anytime.

Mr. Bee became a regular in our pool for the rest of the summer. He was a wonderful man. His wife Barbie Bee was a wonderful lady.

She and my mom, Patricia "Petrinka" Trosk became best friends. There was often nectar, cold and gold, by the pool in the summer of 1981.

Evacuate the Pool!

I was told that I pressed the edges for mom. She wanted sometimes to not be checking diapers yet she had to when I was in the pool. When I got into the pool with mom, she told me later that I had a bad habit of doing my habit right out of the diaper and into the pool.

Mom would be holding me. While she was holding me, I made my habit. Then everybody would have to evacuate the pool for an hour. Mom got the strainer and another bottle of bleach and put it in to sanitize the pool before letting anybody go back in.

Before such an excretory event, apparently, I would always hold onto mom just a little tighter.

That would end the swimming but after an hour the rest of the kids and Mr. Bee were right back in the pool. As I said Mom never let me in the pool alone. She was afraid for my safety and she knew that she had to watch out for diaper-doo.

My dad, Brian Sr. or Brunick as his dad often called him, was most often at work at IBM during the day.

Sometimes he went away for a week or several days for technical seminars. So, he was not with us all the time in the pool.

Dad loved to sing songs in the pool and we would all join him. His favorite song when swimming that first year was the two-line squirrel song which I wrote down for you a while gao.

Everybody enjoyed singing it with him. Dad loved the pool and he loved being with me in the pool. Here is the song again in case you forgot:

This is not a Squirrel Pool

This is a Whirlpool

I would like to jump ahead a few years in this story just for a little while as we are talking about singing. This is a little story about my brother. He was not born until December 30 of this year, 1981. It was not long after he was born that dad and mom both called him Mortrock. He was a definite madcap. He was always into something.

I bring him up now because after a few years, we also sang Mikey's two songs in the pool with dad. He created one of them when in his car seat while on a trip to Boston to see Aunt Sue and Uncle Mitch and he created the other at the Stanton Street Playground while being pushed on the swings.

The Car seat song had one word "Lo." Mikey sang it the best. It went like this

Lo Lo Lo Lo,
Lo Lo Lo Lo
Lo Lo Lo Lo,
Lo Lo Lo Lo.

Sometimes Mike would go on with additional verses using the same word but most of the time, it was just those four lines. Dad and mom really got a kick out of that song.

The song from the Stanton Street Playground that Mike created had a few more words. He called it his bumble bee song and every time he was on the swings, he would sing it with a very happy tone.

Bumble Bee, Who's There? Bumble Bee
Bumble Bee, Who's There? Bumble Bee

Mom and dad and I loved hearing him sing that song too and so we loved it when he would sing it in the pool. When he did, we would all sing along with him. It made us all smile. Sometimes when Mikey sang, dad would say we were all watching *The Mikey Show*.

One more Mikey story before I go back to the pool and the summer of 1981. When we were not in the pool in the summer of 1983, we were either just getting up, going to bed, or it was raining out.

Mom set my letter and number board up in the hallway right outside Dad's office, especially when it was raining.

When Mikey came, dad's office was our bedroom with two bunk beds. Mikey and I were always together.

Mikey had curly hair so much so that Uncle Joe called him the mad professor. Mom could not get herself for a year or more to get him a haircut so that explains that. She thought it was cute.

Anyway, I would love to spell words and by the time Mikey was around, I could form interesting words with my letters using the magnetic board. I loved it.

Dad found out Mikey, who from day one was a great athlete, also liked the letters and numbers for the board.

Dad was coming up the front steps, probably to go to the bathroom as there was just one for the eight-room half-double.

At the bottom he saw a few letters and numbers and he figured I had dropped them when building words on the magnetic board.

He picked them up for me and as he proceeded up the steps on most steps he found a letter or a number or two. Then he looked up the steps.

Mikey was right in front of the gate at the top of the steps with a letter in his hand. He took the letter and like you would skip a rock on a lake he fired the letter with his little hand and it went down the steps and hit dad in the chest.

Mikey loved the letters and I loved the letters but when he was just a little guy, he liked to throw them and I liked to build words out of them. We love each other as brothers for sure but we are different.

This 1985 picture is Mikey and my sister Katie.

Back to the summer of 1981. I hope you liked the diversion about my brother Mikey. I have stories about my sister Katie that I will tell one day. She is very nice, smart, and a great athlete like Mikey. The stork waited another two and a half years to bring her into the world.

Let me say that like Mikey, she loved to swim and she loved to throw things. She is still a great athlete.

By the end of the summer, when I was about 15 months old, I was able to stay afloat in the pool as could Dawn, my best buddie back then. Mom was always in the pool when we were in the pool and Mr. Bee was in there a lot also. Dad would say that I could "tread water."

By the way, I looked up the definition of treading water: "Maintain an upright position in deep water by moving the feet with a walking movement and the hands with a downward circular motion." So there, I did my research.

I was the first child in the Brian W. Kells family to be able to swim. But, then again, in the summer of 1981, my brother Mikey and sister Katie were not born yet.

I remember when mom let me go the first time without the swimmies or the duck tube. I surprised myself even. I was a little scared, I began to move my arms and legs and I was soon in the middle of the pool. I was not sinking. I was almost "swimming." Success! I was treading water. That's about as far as I got in the summer of 1981.

Chapter 10 The Fall of 1981

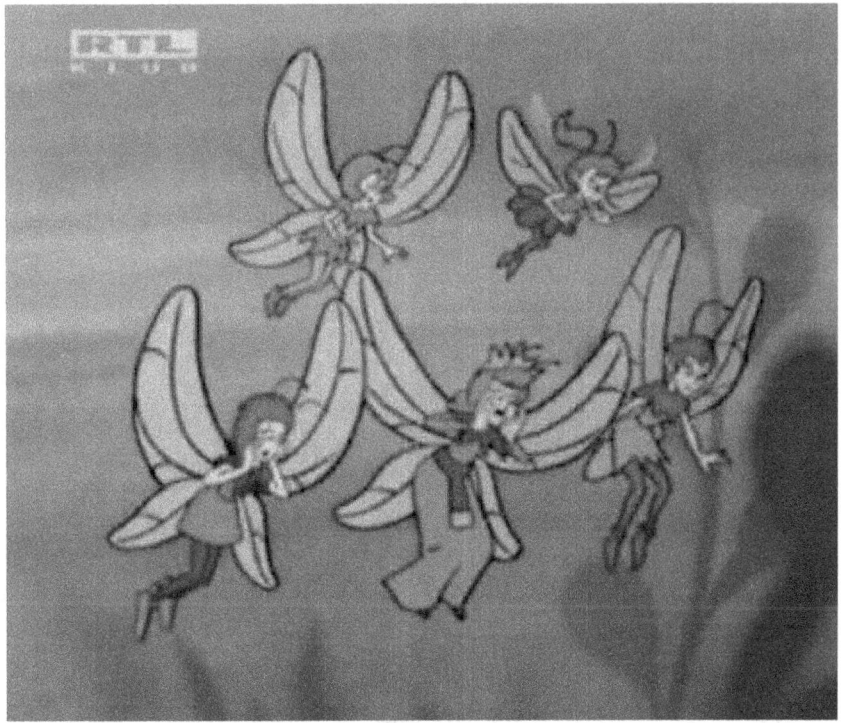

Mom and dad bought a queen-size bed when they moved to the eight-room side of Perfect Street. They put a small TV set in the bedroom but did not watch it very much until I came around.

When there was no need to rush up and get outside since the pool was closed, I soon was big enough that when mom got me out of the crib on Saturday mornings and ahem, after she changed me (shhh!!!), I made the big trip.

She would walk me down the upstairs hallway to the main bedroom and she would put me between dad and her on the queen-sized bed.

We had cable tv and a remote was always handy. There were great kids shows on Saturday Morning. I know I liked Scooby Doo and of course the Smurfs. My dad liked the song about the pixies (shown on prior page) when we watched the Smurfs. Here is the song:

It was called "The Wartmonger Song."

It was a song sung by the three Wartmonger hunters -- Slop, Sludge, and Slime -- in a few Smurfs cartoon show episodes featuring them. Here are the lyrics:

All Three sing:
Oh, we are mighty hunters
In service to the king.
When we go hunting pixies,
We really clip their wings.

Sludge sings:
I'm Sludge the brave.

Slop sings:
I'm Slop the bold.

Slime sings:
I'm Slime the slimy thing.

All Three sing:
When we go hunting pixies,
We really clip their wings, their wings,
Their wingy-wingy-wings.

How can anybody not like that song. Dad loved it. He would sing it at breakfast time after we got up.

Speaking of breakfast, we did not see many, many shows on Saturday morning in bed because we all got hungry and dad would make panapoona. That was dad's word for pancakes. Boy, were they good.

By the fall of 1981, I remember that I could talk and walk but I could not say really big words such as calculator. Dad had a big adding machine on this office desk. As it got colder, I was not outside as much as when the pool was going. I loved that adding machine.

By mid-September, dad had closed up the pool. He said that August was not too bad weather-wise but as soon as Labor Day came, it got too cold to swim.

Dad loved putting me on his lap as he sat in front of his big desk. He had bought it at the Salvation Army for $30.00. He still has it. Dad learned that it had once been used at the Jewish Community Center in Wilkes-Barre.

The desk had a pull-out piece of polished wood with a little handle. When dad pulled it out the sheet of paper said Jewish Community Center on top and it had a list of names and phone extensions according to dad.

Most of the time, Dad had that board stuffed inside his desk. He said he never had to call any of those extensions. Hah!

I guess I got pretty good with the adding machine and I could use it to add and subtract at first. I was not into multiplication or division. Dad also let me use his pocket calculator I loved the calculator. Eventually dad let me have it most of the time.

I loved the calculator, which, before I had begun to speak big words properly, I called the "kuh-shah-shun."

That's the phonetic spelling, of course. Eventually, I could say calculator, just like everybody else, but mom and dad kept using my old word "kuh-shah-shun." because they thought it was so cute.

Dad loves telling the story of a fall 1981 trip to K-Mart. Mom still loves K-Mart. Mom would be shopping and dad would buzz me around the store in the cart.

I loved it when he took me to see the toys, but on this particular trip even dad was surprised. Dad always wore cheap Timex watches so when we got in the store, he was attracted to that part of the store.

He looked at watches for awhile, and did not find any he liked. I was not into watches, so I must have been squirming in the kid's seat of the cart. So, dad decided to take me to see the toys.

As he was pulling out of the watch area, I noticed right next to the watches was a shiny display. It looked like it might be calculators.

Dad's route to the toys passed this counter and as he was passing it, I can recall and dad loves to tell the story that I screamed out:

"kuh-shah-shun."
"kuh-shah-shun."

Dad finally noticed and took me over to see the display models of a bunch of calculators that K-Mart was selling.

Wow! It was like heaven. Dad let me play with all the displayed "kuh-shah-shuns." Then he took me to see the toys. Dad was surprised again that I was so interested in the "kuh-shah-shuns," that I did not care about the toys. I said "kuh-shah-shun" a few more times when we were at the toy aisle.

So on the way out of the store we revisited the calculators and I of course said, "kuh-shah-shun" with a gleam in my eye when we got there. Dad found mom and had to show her. Mom loved it.

I did like those calculators as a little kid. Now I love music and personal computers.

I graduated from Wilkes-University with major honors and a degree in Computer Science. Now, I am a lawyer. I went to Villanova Law School and did quite well. I passed the Bar Exam the first time with a great score. That's quite a big difference from "kuh-shah-shun." to computer science. I also got the Science Award at Wilkes. It was a great honor.

So, that was the great K-Mart "kuh-shah-shun." caper. I can almost remember it. Now we are back to the story and we are about to begin the last couple chapters of this story.

This year, 1981, was my favorite Christmas ever. It was about to be my second Christmas. Before the Christmas holidays were over and before the Christmas stuff was put down the cellar for another year. my brother Mikey was born. That was the greatest. It made me nineteen months older than him.

The neighbors said that Mikey and I were Irish twins. I knew we were Irish with ¼ Polish from Mom, but I never understood the twins part. We were not twins. At least I do not think so. Here is a picture of mom, dad and Mikey in the hospital right after Mikey was born

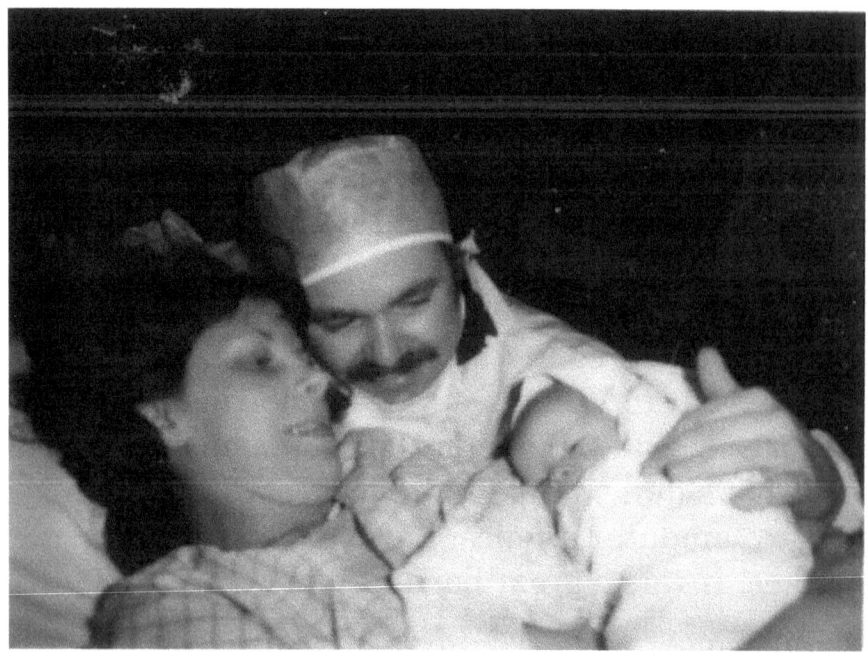

Chapter 11 Baby Brian's Second Christmas

Christmas in 1981 was quite special as I was almost two years old and as I said in Chapter 10, I had developed a great love of calculators, which I called "kuh-shah-shun."

In the Fall, Dad let me use his "kuh-shah-shun," and I had it in my hands almost all the time. Mom bought me another one when she was up at K-Mart some time in November.

When we had a great meal in our Perfect Street kitchen as I was getting older, I would eat big people's food. It was always great, especially mom's spaghetti.

Dad told me I always got a bad case of spaghetti face when I ate spaghetti. Only mom seemed to be able to get those big spaghetti stains off my face.

Dad used after-dinner time and quite frankly any other time, such as when we were in the car to drill me about numbers and letters and words. He loved it and I loved it. It was fun. He also worked with me on the magic magnetic board.

Dad and mom helped me so much with numbers that I could not only count to ten, I could count to 100 long before Christmas that year. Dad would even drill me on counting backwards. By Christmas at 19-months, I could count from 100 backwards and that amazed both mom and dad.

They had me counting for neighbors, friends and relatives. Before Christmas, mom and dad had me adding and subtracting. Sometimes they would give me more than two numbers to work with at a time. I loved numbers and letters. It was great.

In early December, Dad put up the train again and I was mesmerized looking at it as it took shape. As soon as Dad got the train and tree up, just like the year before, he brought out the transformer and taught me how to operate it.

I called the train, the Toot Toot. It was a lot of fun. I could walk pretty good by then and I remember being in the living room looking for the transformer but could never find it. So, I never got to run the train without dad by my side.

I had grown a lot since Christmas 1980, and was big enough that without a booster-chair, I could see the whole platform. I admit that a few times, I did reach in a couple times past the fence and I grabbed an ice skater, or a caroler or a house to get a better look.

Mom was quick even if she was not there to begin with. She would catch me and tell me not to do that and then she would put the figure back where it belonged. She never yelled at me.

This Christmas Eve and Christmas was just like the year before though I don't remember everything about 1980.

The two Pops and Dad went to the Wilkes-Barre Republic Club gala in the afternoon on Christmas Eve. When dad came home, mom had me ready for church and we went early enough to hear the beautiful singing. We started off right away to get to St. Patrick's Church

Mass was more understandable for me this year. It was nice. Mom walked me up to Communion as she received the sacraments with Dad right behind.

After Mass, like the year before mom met the Kennedy's at the back of the church and they chatted. Dad took me to the car hoping mom would get the hint to join us, so we could go to Pop Kells. She did. Then we picked Breezie up at our house. It was all lit up outside from my dad's handiwork. We then packed the car with stuff and drove down to Pop Kells to share gifts.

Grandma Biddie put the Angel Hair on just like the year before and then we got our gifts. It was great. We all had something to drink and then we went up to Pop and Nana Trosk's. We were not the first there but not the last either.

Aunt Mary always helped at Pops.
Looks like an ahem, diaper, in her hand?

Aunt Sue was normally last to arrive at Pop Trosks, as she came in from Boston. Same this year. Pop shared some schnorkies with everybody, sang Silent Night, made everybody cry again and then he ran the train for me and Breezie. Breezie loved the train.

Dad was holding Breezie. Pop called him and he found his three gifts again like as if he was Sherlock Holmes. He opened them one by one on the side. Then all the Trosk siblings exchanged gifts.

Again, they had Swantko's Kielbasa and Russ Swantko, Uncle Stan's buddie from college was there with us. He brought the Kielbasa. Nice!

We had refreshments at Pop Trosks for longer than the year before as everybody was feeling merry. I can recall hearin about somebody who I did not meet, John Jameson. I never met him; but Aunt Sue and dad did. He must have been a chatterbox as we left much later than 1980.

I was getting sleepy some time after midnight and mom said it was time to go. She said we had to hurry to beat Santa Claus to our home.

We got home shortly. Mom and dad tucked me in and then went to bed themselves. They told me Santa was coming overnight. I knew that meant lots of toys. When I fell asleep I was smiling.

Breezie was a big boy again this year and there was no construction under the bed for the second year in a row.

Christmas Morning

In the fall, mom and dad bought bunk beds and moved dad's office to the rear of the house by the bathroom. She had dad make his former office into the boys' room. It was right at the top of the steps. The door was at a diagonal where the front hallway and back hallway and the front stairway met.

We were not sure whether Mikey would be a boy or not but the stork must have told mom something as there was definitely a bed on top of my bed. I had the lower bunk bed. Nobody as of yet was on the top bunk.

I got up early on Christmas Morning and the gate at the top of the steps was locked. It kept me from going downstairs to see what was in the living room by the tree and the toot-toot. I ran into mom and dad's room at the front of the house and they were already up.

They said, Merry Christmas Briney, and gave me a big hug. Do you think Santa was here already, mom said. I said that I sure hope so. Mom got the camera out and we began our trip down the stairs. She was snapping pictures all the while.

I sat midway down the open stairway and I could see a pile of gifts on the floor in the living room. The tree was already lit up. Somehow, dad had the train going already and the tree and train looked beautiful. It was magical for sure. Then, I noticed all the presents by the fireplace paper.

Mom took my picture and then went into the living room and called me. Dad was at the bottom of the steps and he made sure I did not trip and fall down the steps. Soon I was there and the first pile was huge.

Mom said that Santa had left it all for me. Whew! Everything was great. I was thrilled. I opened everything and loved every gift. I thought I was done and was quite pleased when mom said that there was just one more gift that was wrapped very carefully.

I ripped the paper off the box and opened it. It was very light. There was nothing in the box. But then I saw a little note. I could read so I brought out the note and it said:

Check Out TV in Family Room.

I ran into the family room and it was just amazing. Though I was just 19 months old, I had seen computers before connected to TVs in store and in TV commercials but I never thought that I would get one. I still was not sure if it was mine.

Dad said what do you think?

I said "Mine?

He said, "It sure is. Give it a try"

Dad said that the computer was a Texas Instruments TI-99 4A home computer with a voice synthesizer. That meant that in addition to being a computer, the machine could also speak.

It was already hooked up to the TV. Dad said Santa must have done that.

Dad already had loaded a game onto the machine. It was called Hunt the Wumpus.

TI 99 4A Hunt the WUMPUS!

Cartridges for the TI machine were available for kids and adults back then. Does the term: "Hunt the Wumpus" ring a bell?

To anybody reading my story, it sure did then. I could not wait to get at it. Let me tell you a little about it before I tell you what I did next.

Dad told me that *Hunt the Wumpus* was TI's big game for the computer, and it was a lot of fun for families to play together.

There was a box of TI game cartridges that Santa had wrapped in another gift package. Some of the game cartridges were not game cartridges at all.

They were clever little programs which made kids think that learning was fun. For me, it was fun. I was one of those kids.

With the TI, I sure thought learning was a lot of fun. My love of calculators from when I could not even say calculator carried me right to the TI Home Computer.

I was so excited and this was just my second Christmas.

I sure loved my two calculators, which, before I had begun to speak properly, I called my "kuh-shah-shun."

That's the phonetic spelling, of course. Eventually, I could say calculator, just like mom and dad. But, mom and dad kept using "kuh-shah-shun." because they thought it was so cute.

The TI/99 4A Speech Synthesizer was neat!

Anyway. I was about ready to use my new home computer complete with its speech synthesizer. We were in the "gold" room.

First, I got mom and dad to Hunt the Wumpus with me. We got him.

I fell in love with the computer. It was not with the tree and the toot-toot and the toys but it worked while connected to the big TV in the gold family room just a few rooms away from the tree.

I could hear the big LGB train running around the tree platform when I first began to use the TI machine. .

After we played Hunt the Wumpus, mom and dad left me with the computer and they told me they went out to make breakfast.

Before mom and dad knew it, I was sitting down in front of the biggest TV in the house, working one of the math cartridges for kids. I called out to dad to watch me.

I found the cartridge in the box. I read the title and figured out where in the computer it needed to be plugged in and I put it in myself. It worked.

I heard mom say that I was smart like her and Dad said I was smart like him. They both laughed. Hah!

For some reason, the cartridge I picked had math problems—at least for me. They started off with the machine speaking: *"Two plus four plus one equals."* When it finished, it paused and in a deep, slow voice, it said, *"Your turn!"*

Chapter 11 Baby Brian's Second Christmas 115

I quickly "plugged-in" a "7" and the machine rewarded me with a series of happy sounding tunes and small happy fireworks images on the big TV set.

Then the machine said "Twelve plus seventeen plus nine equals." Again, the machine said, in that same deep voice: "Your turn!"

I thought for a while and then I plugged the number in. I knew it was the right answer. As I was plugging in the number, I heard a buzzing and a loud unhappy whirring sound, and the screen was flashing rapidly.

The TI 99 went black and then started the problem again and this time showed me the answer... "38." I knew that I had taken too long to answer.

I was not happy; but I did not quit. I did not want to hear those nasty sounds again.

I already knew the answer but was too late! I had not entered it in time. That would never happen again to me as I knew what I needed to do.

I was just nineteen months old but this stuff came easy for me. I paused the machine and left the room. Mom and dad did not know where I went.

I came back in less than a minute with... you guessed it, my "kuh-shah-shun." The next time the machine said: "Thirteen plus fifteen plus seven,"

While it was talking and showing the numbers on the big TV, I was plugging the numbers into the "kuh-shah-shun" right as it spoke.

When the machine said: "Your turn" I plugged in the value "35" right from the display on the "kuh-shah-shun."

It was great. I heard all the happy music. I had gotten it right. I figured out how to beat the computer. I was never wrong again!

Mom and dad also loved the TI home computer. It seemed like a toy but now I know that for its day, it was as much a computer as the big machines that business people worked with in their offices.

Years later dad explained to me about the TI 99 and he admitted that he and mom got it for me--with Santa's help of course. Ahem! I knew that I loved the math cartridges more than anything else. The voice was something I could not believe.

TI was once the in-home computer champ.

A long time ago, TI made the neatest little computers for families. Dad, who made most of his salaries in life working on big computers, told me that TI parts are still on the inside of a lot of today's technology.

The company was not very good selling in stores however.

One day I saw pictures about a lot of computers in an old book I found called *Thank You, IBM*. My dad had it in his bookshelf. One day I found it. Dad kindly read me some great stories about TI. I did not want to tell dad that by then, I could read. I loved it when dad read to me. Quite frankly, I still do.

I learned that TI was one of the first companies to make digital watches in the 1970s. And we thought that Apple had done that.

He said they made neat stuff. But nothing was as interesting as the TI/99 4A home computer.

In the early 1980's dad said you could buy one for just $50.00 in Northeastern PA at a store known as Boscov's.

At the time, the TI/99 and the 4A version had been available from the late 1970's. For as good as the machines were, TI could not sell (market) them.

When released in 1978, the TI 99 was priced at $1150.00. Later the 4A sold for $525.00. That is still a lot of money, but not when these units were just coming out.

The whole name was the TI/99-4A. Introduced as an enhanced version, this newer machine was more affordable. At $50.00, they were literally a steal. That's how much TI desired to liquidate its inventory.

The "99" and 4A used the same TI-developed speech synthesizer chip unit that would work with many of the TI/99 game cartridges.

From that day on I loved the TI; I loved the Wumpus; and I loved math. I loved Christmas an awful lot also! Yes, I sure did love my mom and dad.

Chapter 12 After Christmas 1981—A New Brother!

Two Great Dinners

Christmas was on a Friday this year, so we had a long weekend. Dad had taken off the whole Christmas season to the end of the year. Because mom was "with child" during the holiday seasons, Dad expected a new little person to be living at 47 Perfect Street by the end of the holy day season.

Anticipating that he would have to help out a lot when the stork brought the new baby, Dad had told his employer, IBM, that if the baby showed up during the holidays, he would be taking two weeks-vacation and then he would be taking every Wednesday off for five more weeks.

Dad said that IBM was always rushing for business to happen around the end of the year but mostly before Christmas.

This was dad's twelfth year with IBM and a lot of years he could not take much vacation during the year as he was asked to work more than he really wanted. He was permitted in his early employment to carry vacation over. He had a lot in reserve when eventually, he retired.

This particular year, he said, just like when the Stork brought me, that would be taking a lot of time off to be with family. He had a lot of time saved up. It was nice having dad home.

After I played with the TI and some other toys Christmas morning, eventually we all ate breakfast. It was still early so I played some more with the toys and the TI and I even was able to run the train by the magical platform.

There were still gifts on the other end of the platform. Mom said that she got dad a few items and Dad had gotten mom a few items. They said they would open them after the flurry of the day.

Soon, mom was getting me all spiffed up to go to Pop and Nana Kells for the early dinner. It was the traditional Turkey with Grandma Biddie's great stuffing. I was eating regular food then and I remember it being great. Breezie was Grandma Biddie's favorite grandson so it seemed. She fed him first and he loved it.

We stayed around Pop Kells s for a few more hours and we all arrived at Pop Trosks at about 3:30 PM. Nana had dinner ready by about 6:30 so we had time to have fun with the family. Below is a picture of Uncle Marty and Aunt Sue.

Pop was out the legion mucking it up with his buddies from the Armed Services. But, he came home in plenty of time for dinner—about 5:00. He turned on the football game and I fell asleep watching it with him and dad and Uncle Marty.

Before I fell asleep Pop ran the HO train for me again and it stayed on the track. That was unusual for

HO trains. It looked like our train but it was about ¼ the size.

The whole Trosk family except Pop and Dad fit around the big dining-room table about 6:30 PM and enjoyed a great Christmas day dinner. There was German Chocolate cake for dessert.

It was all great. I was not too hungry but Nana Trosk (Skippo as Pop called her) said we all had to eat.

We packed up about 8:30 PM and headed for home. There was a lot of excitement. Everybody at the Trosk's was talking to mom about when the baby was coming. I did not really know about a baby, but I noticed mom was a little heavier. Do you think that gave mom's siblings a clue about the stork getting ready to bring a baby? I know I had no clue.

Mom said she did not know "when" but that it would not be Christmas day and more than likely not the next day either.

When we got home, mom took me upstairs and changed me, ahem! She put my PJs on me and tucked me into my lower bunk bed. She told me that soon another baby would be in the house and would be sleeping in the crib that I slept in when I was little.

It was all exciting. I don't remember much more after prayers. Dad would rock me and sing *The Our Father* 'til I fell asleep.

I do recall waking up the next morning hoping somebody would change me, Ahem!

Dad did not bother making plans to go out on New Years' Eve with Mom or to have Good Kaye come over. He figured the stork would come on New Year's Eve. But, asked later, he said he was hoping for more earlier than later.

On December 29, mom was feeling funny. Nana and Pop Kells and Nana and Pop Trosk came to our house to be with me. Dad took mom to the hospital.

Nothing happened on the 29th but on December 30th, the day before New Year's Eve, the grandparents got the call. The stork had brought the baby and it was a boy. His name was Kevin.

Dad stayed with mom 'til she needed to go to sleep. He came home, and the grandparents left but came back the next day early. Dad said to the grandparents that the baby was Kevin when he got home but he changed his mind after a good night sleep. When dad woke up, he said, "Michael is his name." Mom agreed. He did not seem like a Kevin, whatever that is supposed to be.

Dad went back to the hospital and had a very special dinner with mom on New Year's Eve. They told the hospital the baby's name was Michael, On his way home after the dinner with Mom, dad stopped at the Komorek's who were right down the street from Mercy Hospital.

Jim Sheehan was there and dad had a beer or two on this special New Year's Eve before going home. I stayed with Pop and Nana Trosk that night. They were not sure when dad would be home. Dad picked up a pizza from a new place on Barney Street as they were closing on New Year's Eve.

The next day, my new brother, whose name actually was Michael by then, came home. It was January 2. Both Nana and Pop and me were there when Mikey came into the house for the first time. He sure was little.

Here is a picture of Mikey and Mom and Me by the tree the next day after he came home. He is my baby brother.

Chapter 12 After Christmas 1981—A New Brother!

It was pretty busy in the house all week as we enjoyed Mikey and the tree and the toys and the choo choo train. I was hoping it would never end.

On the Thursday after Christmas, January 7, after we all had a nice lunch, Mom put little Mikey up for a nap. She came downstairs in about a half hour. I was playing with the train and I was getting tired.

She took me up for my nap. It was about 1:00 PM in the afternoon.

I did not realize it but the little bit of noise that I heard and the *shhh* sounds when I was falling asleep were very meaningful. While I was napping, mom and dad were putting away all the toys and the platform houses etc.

They also put the train away and took all the ornaments off the tree and they put the tree out at the curb for garbage pickup. Finally, dad unbolted the platforms, disconnected them and took off their legs.

He carried the both platform halves into the cellar one at a time. Mom then ran the sweeper. I kinda heard the sweeper as I often did but I fell back asleep.

At about 4:30 in the afternoon, mom came up and changed me, ahem, again so I could be among the living. Dad was downstairs in the dining-room as I began to come down the steps. Mom was right behind me.

I could not wait to run the train again. Nonetheless, by the time I was about half-way down the steps, I saw nothing in the living-room other than the furniture that was there before the holidays. Mom and dad had put everything away while I was sleeping.

I took a couple more steps to get a better look. My eyes started to well up as I was realizing what had happened. I stopped completely. I looked around and then I put my head down and I said:

No Tree; No Toys; No Toot Toot.

I was so forlorn that I said it again:

No Tree; No Toys; No Toot Toot.

Chapter 13 Life Goes On!

Both mom and dad heard me say:

No Tree! No Toys! No Toot Toot!

I said it in what dad and mom said was the most mournful sounding voice they had ever heard. Mom and dad both told me when I was older that after hearing those words, and in that tone, that they considered putting it all back again. They both said their eyes filled up.

They talked to me afterwards, and quite frankly nobody knows what they said to me to make the hurt go away. None of us to this day are sure.

Eventually, of course, we were all OK. And now, as I approach thirty-nine years of age, I know that there were lots more wonderful Christmases to come.

There were lots more decorated trees over the years. There were lots more toys. And, of course there was a Toot Toot to play with every single year.

When we moved from Perfect Street after thirteen years, having had Dawn, the Callahans and our other buddies to play with; we had what mom called a Sun Room. It was 21' X 16'. It had a high cathedral ceiling. It is still there, and it is neat.

Dad and Ralph, cousin Erin's buddy, built a ten-inch shelf that was about eight feet off the ground—all around the Sun Room. He painted the shelf white. He bought enough LGB (Lehman Gross Bahn) track to go all the way around the Sun Room on that shelf.

He then put the track up on the shelf and connected the transformer wires to it, At the corner of the far side of the Sun Room, he poked a hole in the shelf and he connected the wires to the transformer and put the transformer in a cabinet that was below the shelf.

He used an 8-foot ladder to put the LGB train engine and all the cars on the track. Then dad tried it out. It worked well. It also worked in reverse and it sped across the tracks very quickly all around the Sun Room.

I was eight years old when we moved. Dad would take me out into the Sun Room as often as I wanted. I would then operate the train (Toot Toot) for almost as long as I wanted.

Mikey was also old enough when we moved from Perfect Street, and dad taught him to run the train. In another year, Katie was running the train also. The *Toot Toot* was back for good.

What a wonderful *Toot Toot*, wonderful toys, and Wonderful Trees. I'll never forget. Thank you mom and dad. Thank you God for giving me my mom and dad and Mikey and Katie and of course, my best buddy Dawn, who we also called Dinder.

My life has been one glorious moment after another. I love my mom and dad , brother and sister, aunts and uncles and cousins and great friends like Dawn, and Jackie and Shannon to pieces and that is that.

A few Extra Pictures.

My second Christmas season on Perfect street saw the stork bring me a baby brother (Mikey) and then in about two and a half years, that same stork (I think) brought me a baby sister (Katie). It was wonderful. Now I know why Adam needed Eve to complete his life. We all need good friends and relatives and people to love.

As I grew older, I was much happier having Mikey and Katie and Dawn in my life than all the wonder I experienced with the Tree, the Toys, and even the Toot Toot. What a great life.

When I was trying to find memorable pictures to help me better tell my story, I found some that I did not need and some that I wish I could have more than one-of so I could better tell the story of so many wonderful Christmases.

So, if it is OK with you, I am going to put those pictures in this chapter of the book. They show me of course, mom and dad, the platform, and they show Mikey and Katie. I was so glad to show Dawn earlier in the book. I hope you like them all.

On this page, you will find a picture of the most wonderful lady in my life. I am sure Mikey, and Katie and Dad feel the same. In the picture, you will find mom, me, Mikey, and Katie in the second-last year that we lived on Perfect Street. Isn't mom beautiful?

Though the picture below is not very clear, I put it in this story because it shows my dad and how thrilled he was to be the father of the Kelly Kids, including Katie, Mikey, & Me. Here is a picture of Me and Mike and Dad. He liked wearing jeans along with a sport coat that he always called his stomping jacket.

Katie was born in 1984 but the picture on this page is from 1985 as Katie was born November 12, 1984. She was less than two months when she made it through the holiday as you can see in Mom's great picture in the open stairway on Perfect Street.

For Mikey and my first Christmas together when I was three and he was one; mom actually sewed little suits by hand. Dad could not believe how nice they were.

Look at pictures of Mikey when you have a chance. Even I love Mikey's hair when I see it in these early pictures. I bet that mom sewed Katie's little outfit that she wore in this picture below:

Dad loved that mom sewed such wonderful outfits for us so much that one year, he gave a special present to Mom. He put a huge red bow on a huge box. Mom loved it. It was a brand-new Singer Sewing Machine and it was already mounted in a desk unit to make it easier for mom to sew if she wished. She's looking right at it in this picture below:

Mom and dad were well known by our cousins for throwing great kids' parties. In the circa 1982 picture on the next page, there are a ton of wonderful little ones without Katie, who was not born yet. They are the wonderful Kells and Trosk cousins that I talk about in the stories.

See the picture below. From the back, there is mom and Mikey and to mom's left is me on Aunt Sue's lap. Matt and Alie were not born yet. Then, there is Meghan and Liz Danells, and on the front left—Unce Joe with Tara, who was Mikey's good buddy at the time. Moving completely around the table, I see Justin, and two other buddies, David and Kenny Flanders. Justin must have bullied Peph out of the pic. Look how fun the table looks. That is my mom. Don't you love her already.

Look at the back door of the Kells house on Perfect Street. Outside that door, for many years until 1987, the many kids at the table and more would egress out to the pool deck where even more fun could be had. The mugs on the left wall were dad's from many years of beer snuggling.

Look at Uncle Joe on the very left front in this picture.

Now, this is the same handsome uncle Joe holding Mikey in the picture below. Mikey's favorite cousin in the early years was Tara. She is uncle Joe and Aunt Diane's baby daughter. No Colleen yet! Tara and Mikey are the same age. They have always been best of buddies. I think that is Aunt Di holding Tara.

If this were a cartoon, I would now say That's All Folks! But instead let me remind you that the reason that I wrote this great big story is because my mom and dad have told me so many times about a part of the story that would be titled, No Tree, No Toys; No Toot-Toot. Somebody had to tell it correctly. After all, I am the nineteen-month-old who first said those words:

No Tree! No Toys. No Toot Toot!---- And, so,

That's All Folks! Doesn't it get you right here ?

Other Books by Brian W. Kelly: (amazon.com, and Kindle)

Government Must Stop Ripping Off Seniors' Social Security!: Hey buddy, seniors can no longer spare a dime?
Special Report: Solving America's Student Debt Crisis!: The only real solution to the $1.52 Trillion debt
How to End DACA, Sanctuary Cities, & Resident Illegal Aliens . best solution to wipe shadows in America.
The Winning Political Platform for America A unique winning approach to solve the big problems in America.
Lou Barletta v Bob Casey for US Senate Barletta has a unique approach to solving the big problems in America.
John Chrin v Matt Cartwright for Congress Chrin has a unique approach to solving big problems in America.
The Cure for Hate !!! Can the cure be any worse than this disease that is crippling America?
Andrew Cuomo's Time to Go? "He Was Never that Great!": Cuomo says America never that great
White People Are Bad! Bad! Bad! Whoever thought a popular slogan in 2018 would be *It's OK to be White!*
The Fake News Media Is Also Corrupt !!!: Fake press / media today is not worthy to be 4th Estate.
God Gave US Donald Trump?   Trump was sent from God as the people's answer
Millennials Say America Was "Never That Great": Too many pleased days of political chumps not over!
White People Are Bad! Bad! Bad! In 2018, too many people find race as a non-equalizer.
It's Time for The John Doe Party… Don't you think? By By Elephants.
Great Players in Florida Gators Football… Tim Tebow and a ton of other great players
Great Coaches in Florida Gators Football… The best coaches in Gator history.
The Constitution by Hamilton, Jefferson, Madison, et al. The Real Constitution
The Constitution Companion. Will help you learn and understand the Constitution
Great Coaches in Clemson Football The best Clemson Coaches right to Dabo Swinney
Great Players in Clemson Football The best Clemson players in history
Winning Back America. America's been stolen and can be won back completely
The Founding of America… Great book to pick up a lot of great facts
Defeating America's Career Politicians. The scoundrels need to go.
Midnight Mass by Jack Lammers… You remember what it was like Great story
The Bike by Jack Lammers… Great heartwarming Story by Jack
Wipe Out All Student Loan Debt--Now! Watch the economy go boom!
No Free Lunch Pay Back Welfare! Why not pay it back?
Deport All Millennials Now!!! Why they deserve to be deported and/or saved
DELETE the EPA, Please! The worst decisions to hurt America
Taxation Without Representation 4th Edition Should we throw the TEA overboard again?
Four Great Political Essays by Thomas Dawson
Top Ten Political Books for 2018… Cliffnotes Version of 10 Political Books
Top Six Patriotic Books for 2018… Cliffnotes version of 6 Patriotic Boosk
Why Trump Got Elected!.. It's great to hear about a great milestone in America!
The Day the Free Press Died. Corrupt Press Lives on!
Solved (Immigration) The best solutions for 2018
Solved II (Obamacare, Social Security, Student Debt) Check it out; They're solved.
Great Moments in Pittsburgh Steelers Football... Six Super Bowls and more.
Great Players in Pittsburgh Steelers Football ,,,Chuck Noll, Bill Cowher, Mike Tomin, etc.
Great Coaches in New England Patriots Football,,, Bill Belichick the one and only plus others
Great Players in New England Patriots Football… Tom Brady, Drew Bledsoe et al.
Great Coaches in Philadelphia Eagles Football..Andy Reid, Doug Pederson & Lots more
Great Players in Philadelphia Eagles Football Great players such as Sonny Jurgenson
Great Coaches in Syracuse Football All the greats including Ben Schwartzwalder
Great Players in Syracuse Football. Highlights best players such as Jim Brown & Donovan McNabb
Millennials are People Too !!! Give US millennials help to live American Dream
Brian Kelly for the United States Senate from PA: Fresh Face for US Senate
The Candidate's Bible. Don't pray for your campaign without this bible
Rush Limbaugh's Platform for Americans… Rush will love it
Sean Hannity's Platform for Americans… Sean will love it
Donald Trump's New Platform for Americans. Make Trump unbeatable in 2020
Tariffs Are Good for America! One of the best tools a president can have
Great Coaches in Pittsburgh Steelers Football Sixteen of the best coaches ever to coach in pro football.
Great Moments in New England Patriots Football Great football moments from Boston to New England
Great Moments in Philadelphia Eagles Football. The best from the Eagles from the beginning of football.
Great Moments in Syracuse Football The great moments, coaches & players in Syracuse Football
Boost Social Security Now! Hey Buddy Can You Spare a Dime?
The Birth of American Football. From the first college game in 1869 to the last Super Bowl
Obamacare: A One-Line Repeal Congress must get this done.
A Wilkes-Barre Christmas Story A wonderful town makes Christmas all the better
A Boy, A Bike, A Train, and a Christmas Miracle A Christmas story that will melt your heart
Pay-to-Go   America-First Immigration Fix

Legalizing Illegal Aliens Via Resident Visas Americans-first plan saves $Trillions. Learn how!
60 Million Illegal Aliens in America!!! A simple, America-first solution.
The Bill of Rights By Founder James Madison Refresh *your knowledge of the specific rights for all*
Great Players in Army Football Great Army Football played by great players..
Great Coaches in Army Football Army's coaches are all great.
Great Moments in Army Football Army Football at its best.
Great Moments in Florida Gators Football Gators Football from the start. This is the book.
Great Moments in Clemson Football CU Football at its best. This is the book.
Great Moments in Florida Gators Football Gators Football from the start. This is the book.
The Constitution Companion. A Guide to Reading and Comprehending the Constitution
The Constitution by Hamilton, Jefferson, & Madison – Big type and in English
PATERNO: The Dark Days After Win # 409. Sky began to fall within days of win # 409.
JoePa 409 Victories: Say No More! Winningest Division I-A football coach ever
American College Football: The Beginning From before day one football was played.
Great Coaches in Alabama Football Challenging the coaches of every other program!
Great Coaches in Penn State Football the Best Coaches in PSU's football program
Great Players in Penn State Football The best players in PSU's football program
Great Players in Notre Dame Football The best players in ND's football program
Great Coaches in Notre Dame Football The best coaches in any football program
Great Players in Alabama Football from Quarterbacks to offensive Linemen Greats!
Great Moments in Alabama Football AU Football from the start. This is the book.
Great Moments in Penn State Football PSU Football, start--games, coaches, players,
Great Moments in Notre Dame Football ND Football, start, games, coaches, players
Cross Country with the Parents A great trip from East Coast to West with the kids
Seniors, Social Security & the Minimum Wage. Things seniors need to know.
How to Write Your First Book and Publish It with CreateSpace. You too can be an author.
The US Immigration Fix--It's all in here. Finally, an answer.
I had a Dream IBM Could be #1 Again The title is self-explanatory
WineDiets.Com Presents The Wine Diet Learn how to lose weight while having fun.
Wilkes-Barre, PA; Return to Glory Wilkes-Barre City's return to glory
Geoffrey Parsons' Epoch... The Land of Fair Play Better than the original.
The Bill of Rights 4 Dummmies! This is the best book to learn about your rights.
Sol Bloom's Epoch …Story of the Constitution The best book to learn the Constitution
America 4 Dummmies! All Americans should read to learn about this great country.
The Electoral College 4 Dummmies! How does it really work?
The All-Everything Machine Story about IBM's finest computer server.
ThankYou IBM! This book explains how IBM was beaten in the computer marketplace by neophytes

Amazon.com/author/brianwkelly
Brian W. Kelly has written 182 books.
Thank you for buying this one.

www.ingramcontent.com/pod-product-compliance
Lightning Source LLC
Chambersburg PA
CBHW070641050426
42451CB00008B/254